Accepting the YOKE *of* HEAVEN

COMMENTARY ON THE WEEKLY TORAH PORTION

Accepting the
YOKE of
HEAVEN

COMMENTARY ON THE
WEEKLY TORAH PORTION

Yeshayahu Leibowitz

translated by Shmuel Himelstein

URIM PUBLICATIONS

NEW YORK • JERUSALEM

To Grete

Accepting the Yoke of Heaven: Commentary on the Weekly Torah Portion
by Professor Yeshayahu Leibowitz
Translator and Editor: Rabbi Dr. Shmuel Himelstein
Previously published with the title: Notes and Remarks on the Weekly Parasha
Copyright © 2002, 1990 by Chemed Books and Co. Inc.

Second Edition
ISBN 965-7108-33-0

Urim Publications, P.O. Box 52287, Jerusalem 91521 Israel

Lambda Publishers Inc.
3709 13th Avenue Brooklyn, New York 11218 U.S.A.
Tel: 718-972-5449 Fax: 718-972-6307
Email: mh@ejudaica.com

www.UrimPublications.com

CONTENTS

CHUMASH VAYIKRA

CHUMASH BAMIDBAR

CHUMASH DEVARIM

INTRODUCTORY NOTE

In the yearly cycle of the Torah reading on *Shabbat*, from *Shabbat Bereishit* in the year 5746 (1985) to *Simchat Torah* 5747 (1986), I was given the honor—by the Israeli Educational Television and by *Galei Zahal*, the IDF radio station—to offer talks on the weekly *sidra*. For this, I was allotted 15 minutes each Friday afternoon, which, after subtracting the introductory remarks by the announcer, left me between 12 and 13 minutes of air time.

Within this framework of 49 weekly broadcasts on the 54 *sidrot* (on some weeks two *sidrot* are combined) and on *Kohelet* (Ecclesiastes), I had no intention of teaching *Chumash* or of explaining the Torah in accordance with one of the traditional ways of —פרד״ס *peshat*, the literal meaning; *remez*, by allusion or hint; *derash*, through homiletical expansion; or *sod*, in the hidden or mystical sense; or in accordance with the Midrash and Aggada. Nor did I follow scientific research or my own personal interpretations (even though each person has the right to offer *derash* as he sees fit, "the gates of *derash* never having been closed"). Nor was I able to offer a survey of the entire *sidra* in terms of its content, its narrative and its *mitzvot* (commandments). All I intended to do each time was to comment on one of the many topics contained in each *sidra*, on one of its aspects, on one of its verses, or even on a single word within it, or on a comment found in the midrashic literature or in the traditional commentaries—on a detail which appeared to me to be worthy of attention and which drew me to comment. Even in those matters in which I was preceded by others, and in which I had nothing innovative to offer, I had no hesitation in repeating and clarifying them, if it appeared to me that it was worth doing so because the matter had not been stressed sufficiently.

The 49 talks did not proceed from an overall master plan, and there was no fixed method in choosing the topics for the talks. The talks were given as I felt each time, sometimes in accordance with what I knew about a specific topic, sometimes in terms of the connection between a given topic and others in the Torah, or in regard to what was said or written about the Torah, and sometimes in accordance with the association with current events. Generally, I planned to relate more to topics of faith rather than to historical or philological topics. The broadcasts were given in the form of free talks, in most cases without any preparation in writing, which explains some of the features of style and formulation. Each week, the talk was transcribed from the broadcast film of Educational Television to one of the Israeli dailies.

This series of broadcasts evoked a lively response from viewers and listeners. Each week I would receive, by mail or by phone, comments or questions regarding what had been said in the broadcast, requests for clarification of items that had not been explained sufficiently within the quarter-hour framework, or even requests to enable the talks to be read. It was therefore decided that they would be published in the form of a book.

But, as is known, oral discourse is different than the printed word, along the lines of the words of our Sages: "Those things which are oral may not be written by you" (the reference here is to the relationship between the oral and the written Torah). One may therefore note that the material brought to the attention of the reader requires a more exact and accurate formulation than does the oral transmission of the talks. The language of the broadcasts therefore needed a certain stylistic correction. So too was it necessary to cut down on those ideas which were repeated in a number of broadcasts—because on occasion there were months separating the discussion of the same topic in two different *sidrot*, where the words might have been forgotten—whereas in a book they are all open to the perusal of the reader. Moreover, in certain instances, there are clarifications in the written text to what were mere allusions in the limited time of the broadcasts, where these were not explained fully. In general, though, I refrained from editing the material in a way that would alter its character from a series of remarks and notes to a systematic exposition; and that is the style in which the talks are brought before the reader.

I wish to express my gratitude to Yael Zadok (of Educational Television), who gave the opening remarks before each talk; also to Pazit Fein (of the daily *Chadashot*), who took care to print the broadcasts in her newspaper. In the editing of this work, I was aided by my wife, Dr. Grete Leibowitz, who offered advice on a number of corrections and in reading the proofs. Finally, my student—comrade, Ephraim Yaakov, devoted a great deal of time in gathering the material, proofreading it, and in bringing the corrected material to the press.

Yeshayahu Leibowitz
Erev Shavuot 5748 (1988)

Note on the Translation

The translator, Rabbi Dr. Shmuel Himelstein, devoted much effort in conveying the specific topics and terms of the world of Jewish thought. At times, a literal translation was simply impossible; and in those instances, the topic had to, by necessity, be rewritten in a form that differed from the Hebrew original. In these difficult instances, there was fruitful cooperation between myself and the translator, and I owe a debt of deep gratitude to Dr. Himelstein for making the English version of this book available to the reader.

Yeshayahu Leibowitz
Tu Beshvat 5749 (1989)

CHUMASH

BEREISHIT

BEREISHIT

The Torah commences with seven mighty Hebrew words, which are translated as, "In the beginning, God created heaven and earth." What does this verse indicate? This question has been deliberated upon throughout the generations by the different commentators. Regardless of whether they interpreted the Torah according to its literal meaning, its interpretation, allegorically or mystically, all of them attempted to understand both the literal meaning or the conceptual meaning contained in this verse. As true believers, they all recognized the Torah as a demand made upon man to serve God, the implication of this for man being the acceptance of the Yoke of Heaven as embodied in the Yoke of the Torah and the *mitzvot*— commandments. But the presentation of this demand and its realization, in the form of the *mitzvot*, is contained within a narrative framework, which begins with the creation of the world and the commencement of the history of mankind.

What does the *sidra* of *Bereishit* add to that demand, and what does it contribute to its realization? This question faced the greatest meditators on the Torah in terms of faith. Maimonides makes a considerable effort to free the comprehension of God (that precisely being the acceptance of the Yoke of Heaven) from dependence on specific information (the eternity of the universe as opposed to its creation at a certain time). Nachmanides, on the other hand, sees belief in the creation of the world at a specific time as a condition for belief in God. In order to impart to the story of the creation a religious significance which is beyond its cosmological content, a Midrash—on the verse which commences the repetition of the story of the creation, "This is the story of heaven and earth when they were created" (*Bereishit* 2:4)—notes that the Hebrew for "when they were created"—בהבראם contains the same letters as אברהם Abraham. This indicates, says the Midrash, that it was for the sake of Abraham that heaven and earth were created. What this conveys is that the whole purpose of heaven and earth is to serve as the background for the man who was the first of whom it was stated clearly: "he believed in God."

The entire narrative framework is but the background for the embodiment of faith in the form of that man who arose early in the morning, saddled his ass, and took his son Isaac, together with fire and a slaughtering knife, and who "arose and went to the place where God had told him." On Abraham's saddling up of his ass (*chamor* in Hebrew), Abarbanel comments: "He overcame the physical (*chomriut* in Hebrew) within himself"—a victory of the spirit over nature.

Yet the first *parasha* of *Bereishit* deals specifically with physical nature, with heaven and earth and all their hosts, with the inanimate, the animate, and man himself. Why is this so? It is commonly known that *Rashi* commences his commentary on the Torah by presenting a question asked earlier by the Midrash: If the primary purpose of the Torah is to have the Jewish people accept upon itself the service of God as embodied in the *mitzvot*, why doesn't the Torah begin with the first *mitzva* given to Israel, which is only to be found in the Book of Exodus (it is true that there are a number of *mitzvot* that are either alluded to, or stated outright, in Genesis, but these were not *mitzvot* to the Jewish people, for only when it left Egypt was it consolidated into a nation upon which was imposed the obligation to observe the Torah)? It is also widely known that *Rashi* does not give a factual answer to this question, but rather resorts to a midrashic one, an answer that one might almost consider to be folkloristic.

The *sidra* of *Bereishit* was not given to impart to us information on the world and all in it, but was directed at the historical future, in order to provide the basis for the right of the Jewish people to the Land of Israel, as opposed to the claim by the other nations of the world: "You are a nation of brigands, for you stole the land of the Seven Nations (of Cana'an)." The answer to this is, "In the beginning, God created heaven and earth"—no human group owns the land, "for earth is God's and all that is in it," and He does with it as He sees fit; it was His will to give it to the Canaanites first, and it was at His will that He took it from the Canaanites and gave it to Israel. We all know that similar claims are heard today from the mouths of believing Jews as the basis for their stance on major contemporary problems, in the debates between Israel and the other nations.

But one must be very careful in using the categories of midrashic interpretation of the Torah as the basis for positions which reflect political needs and interests. This can be a two-edged sword to those involved. If we continue along the lines which *Rashi* derives from the Midrash, we will be forced to say: Of course "the earth is God's and all that is in it"—and therefore, when He desired to, He took Cana'an from the Canaanites and gave it to Israel; and when He desired to, He took it from the Jewish people and gave it to the Romans; and when He desired to, He took it from the Romans and gave it to the Arabs; and when He desired to, He took it from the Arabs and gave it to the Crusaders; and when He desired to, He took it from the Crusaders and gave it to the Mameluks; and when He desired to, He took it from the Mameluks and gave it to the Turks; and when He desired to, He took it from the Turks and gave it to the British—and we again appear as litigants. The deep significance of that Midrash is that no nation has the right to any land, for the owner of all the land is God.

And from the Midrash to the conceptual content of the verse: What is the meaning of the seven Hebrew words translated as "In the beginning God created heaven and earth"? Is this information about an event that took place at a certain specific time? If so, why does it state בראשית, which, translated literally, means "in the beginning *of?*" The beginning of what? The beginning of time? We are immediately confronted with one of the greatest of problems, possibly the greatest of all, in metaphysical thought: the problem of time and the concept of the beginning of time, or—in the more comprehensive sense—the concept of the beginning of reality. Is one able to give this meaning within the categories of human thought? All philosophical attempts to grapple with this, from ancient times to the present, result in antinomies. Or are we to say that "the beginning" referred to here is not a concept of time at all, but rather expresses a cause or source?

The second Hebrew word too, "created"—what does it mean? The human categories are: made, built, formed, shaped; we are not familiar with the category of "created" within our reality and in the world with which we are familiar. (Late) theological thought explains this as the producing of something from nothing. This concept, too, is not rational, and in any event we have no certainty that this is the literal meaning of the verse (Ibn Ezra questions it). There is no doubt that "created" expresses a relationship between God and the world—but what is the nature of that relationship, which we are unable to understand, let alone visualize? Thus we see that the first two words do not supply man with any information on any event. The first verse in the Torah presents the great principle of faith: the world is not God—as opposed to any other outlook which exists in human culture: as opposed to paganism, whose gods belong to the world and are to be found in the world; as opposed to Christianity, which at first blush received from Judaism the concept of the transcendent God, but immediately attired it in a human form which existed in the world; and as opposed to atheism, for which the world is the totality of being, or, in other words, that it is God. As opposed to all of these, the Torah says, "In the beginning, God created heaven and earth"; the world is not God, and God is not in the world—God is beyond the world, beyond any reality to which man's concepts are bound, and beyond the needs and the interests which stem from man's existence in the world. Neither the world nor man is prime; God is not for the world, as with the Platonic demiurge; and He is not for man. Rather, God is prime, and the world (including man in it) is subordinate. And this is the way this was phrased at a later period in the *siddur*: "You were You before the world was created, and You are You since the world was created." The creation mentioned in the *sidra* of *Bereishit* rejects every naturalistic and humanistic viewpoint in favor of faith in God.

NOACH

Whenever one mentions the *sidra* of *Noach*, it understandably brings to mind the flood. But there are times when people ignore the fact that the *sidra* is composed of two different sections. Only the first section deals with the flood; the second is about the world after the flood, that being the world we live in today. It is an interesting fact that the dividing line between these two worlds dissects the exact middle of the *sidra*. The first 77 verses deal with the flood, while the 76 verses after the verse, "this is the sign of the covenant" (*Bereishit* 9:17), refer to our world. The covenant mentioned here is the promise that the world will continue to exist, with nature remaining as it is now, unlike the previous world, whose nature would change as a result of the flood. From that point on, the world continues according to its standard pattern: "seedtime and harvest, and cold and heat, and summer and winter, and day and night will not cease" (*Bereishit* 8:22). This is the world in which we live.

Now, in appraising these two worlds, it would appear that there is no difference between them. Regarding man before the flood, we are told, "every inclination of [man's] thoughts was always evil" (*Bereishit* 6:5), whereas after the flood it states, "for the inclination of man's heart is evil from his youth upwards" (8:21). The condition of the earth before the flood was one of, "the earth was corrupt...and the earth was filled with violence" (*Bereishit* 6:11), and the world after the flood begins with drunkenness and lewdness, followed by the Tower of Bavel, or, as our Sages refer to it, the generation of the separation. It is with the Tower of Bavel that I would like to deal today.

If one reads the text superficially, it would appear that this deals with a sin by mankind, and the punishment which followed it. However, if we examine the matter in depth, we will see that there was no comparison between the generation of the flood and the generation of the separation. Regarding the generation of the flood, we are told clearly, "all flesh had corrupted its way on the earth" (*Bereishit* 6:12)—and the flood came as a punishment. Regarding the generation of the separation, the Torah merely mentions that they planned to construct a city and a tower, and to congregate about this structure. There is no specific statement in the Torah deploring this, but as a result of this action, God decreed that the languages be convoluted, and that people be dispersed throughout the world. Again, superficially, it would appear to us that the decree came about as a punishment, but this is not stated specifically.

It would appear to me that this decree was not a punishment, but, on the contrary, it was an action taken for the benefit of mankind. The major significance of the Tower of Bavel episode is not at all the attempt to construct a tower, but refers back to what is stated earlier, that "the whole earth—the renewed mankind after the flood—was of one language and of one speech" (*Bereishit* 11:1). After the failure of the construction, different languages arose, and that entailed different speech. It appears to me that the root of the error, or sin, of the generation of the separation was not the building of a city and tower, but the aim to use these artificial means to ensure a situation of "one language and one speech"—of centralization, which, in modern parlance, would be known as totalitarianism. One language and one speech is, according to many naive people in our days, a description of an ideal situation: all of humanity a single bloc, without differentiation, and, as a result, without conflicts. But one who truly understands will know that there is nothing which is more threatening than this artificial conformism: a city and tower as the symbol of the concentration of all of mankind about a single topic—where there will be no differences of opinion and where there will be no struggle over different viewpoints and values. One cannot imagine greater tyranny than that, one cannot imagine a greater mental and moral sterility than that—that there should be no exceptions and that there should be no deviations from what is accepted and agreed upon, and this being maintained by the artificial means of a city and a tower.

In His mercy and compassion for mankind, God prevented this from occurring, and He made a humanity where a totalitarianism of complete unity cannot be. Thus, there are differences and contrasts, differentiation of thought and differentiation of values, in which people have to struggle for their values, for their aims, and for their desires which differ one from the other.

It is true that the result is that human history has been such that one of the greatest historians stated that it is nothing but the account of the crimes, follies and disasters of the human species. This historian (Edward Gibbon) told the truth, but did not tell the whole truth. It is true that history is the account of the crimes, follies and disasters, but it is also the account of the struggle of people against the crimes, against the follies, and against the disasters, and the fact that this struggle exists in all times and in all human societies is what grants moral significance to the history of mankind.

It is not coincidental that only after the episode of the Tower of Bavel, when there was no longer "one language" and there was no longer "one speech" for all of mankind, was Abraham able to arise and to revolt against the world of his father Terach and his idols (according to the Aggada, he also revolted against Nimrod the Wicked's rule). In a world of "one language and one speech," an Abraham can never arise against Terach (and Nimrod). God granted us a great favor, in that He prevented the totalitarian concentration of people, and permitted—and even forced—them to struggle over conceptions and values, even if this struggle involves heavy sacrifices, but sacrifices of importance.

One of the great Jewish Sages of a later period of time (R. Akiva) said, on the verse, "the years draw near, when you will say, I see no purpose in them" (*Kohelet* 12:1)—which according to the literal meaning refers to man's old age—that this is a hint at the messianic age, "when there will be neither merit nor guilt": in a world in which all the problems have been solved and there is perfect harmony, where there are no good deeds or bad deeds, and where there is no place for struggles and efforts, there will be "no purpose in them." The "purpose" we can discern in existence consists just in the differentiation—in contrasting viewpoints and differences over which people struggle, and over which they battle, and it is by this that their existence gains moral value.

LEKH LEKHA

Our forefather Abraham is mentioned for the first time in the concluding verses of the *sidra* of *Noach*. The *sidrot* of *Lekh Lekha* and *Vayera* are the prime *sidrot* dealing with his life. Afterwards, in *Chayye Sarah*, we only have Abraham's last days: the death of Sarah, his son Isaac's marriage, and Abraham's death. We have therefore decided to devote this talk to both *Lekh Lekha* and *Vayera*, even though, when we get to *Vayera*, we will deal with the *sidra* on its own. The framework dealing with Abraham's life is symbolized and marked by identical words at its beginning and at its end: it is as if an arch is stretched over the 250 verses from, "Get you (*lekh lekha*) out of your country, and from your kindred, and from your father's house" (*Bereishit* 12:1), to, "Get you (*lekh lekha*) to the land of Moriah...upon one of the mountains of which I will tell you" (22:2).

The first *lekh lekha* was meant to have Abraham come to the designated land, while the second signified Abraham's going to the *Akeida*.

Abraham progresses from the one *lekh lekha* to the other, that being the path of *emuna*—faith. Between the two *lekh lekha*'s, there are two verses, one in the *sidra* of *Lekh Lekha* and the other in that of *Vayera*, which indicate the significance of this path. Already in *Lekh Lekha*, we are told about Abraham—and he is the first person of which the Torah says this—"He believed in God" (*Bereishit* 15:6). Further, in *Vayera*, it states, "Now I know that you fear God" (*Bereishit* 22:12). This gives us reason to pause: If already at the very outset—when he was still known as Abram—the Torah praises

Abraham so highly with the words, "He believed in God," what is the significance of the episode in *Vayera*, where we are told, "After this, God put Abraham to the test" (*Bereishit* 22:1)? Why did He test him—after all, the Torah has already testified that he believed in God! Rather, the faith in *Lekh Lekha* refers to God's words, "Fear not, Abram: I am your shield, and your reward is exceedingly great...and he believed in God." We ask: What did Abraham believe in? From the text of this verse, it would follow that Abraham believed in God's protection and the reward which he was promised. But did he believe in God? And these are two very different matters.

Here I cannot resist telling of a certain person in our midst, of a very high intellectual and moral caliber, who is also immersed in Judaism, who said that after Auschwitz he lost his faith in God. My response to this is: you never believed in God but in God's help, and that faith was disillusioned—God did not help. One who believes in God, however, does not relate this to belief in God's help; nor does he expect that God will help him. He believes in God in terms of His Godhead, not in terms of the functions that he attributes to Him concerning His dealing with man. And that is the significance of the *Akeida*, in which God appears to Abraham, not as He who protects him and not as He who rewards him, but as He who makes the most difficult and exacting of demands, a demand that he is unable to fulfill unless he nullifies all human needs, interests and values— nullifying them in order to serve God.

Abraham withstood this test, and that is why only then was he told, "Now I know that you fear God." Indeed, there are two types of fear of God—there is the fear of God based on what the person expects or fears in terms of what God will do to him, and there is the fear of God which is but the awe of His majesty: the person fears God because of His being God and not because of a function which he attributes to Him in regard to man. That is the significance of the life story of Abraham in the two *sidrot* of *Lekh Lekha* and *Vayera*: from the man who feared the God who had promised him the land and promised a great future for his descendants, to the man who saddled the ass, took along his son, the fire and a slaughtering knife, and went to fulfill God's command, which would entail the nullification of all of God's promises.

The long road from the first *lekh lekha* to the second is the event-filled life of Abraham, who, as the Midrash tells us, "was tested ten times." It was a life of wandering—from Aram Naharayim to Cana'an, from Cana'an to Egypt, and back from Egypt to Cana'an; and even in Cana'an he "went on his journeys," "journeying and going on" from one place to the next, dwelling in Beit El, then in Gerar, then in Be'er Sheva, then in Chevron. On his journeys, he experienced all the concerns that one has in life, both in one's personal life and one's public life: questions of property and acquiring ownership, questions concerned with relations between man and wife, as well as social and political matters—Abraham concluded a treaty with Canaanite friends, but also waged war and concluded a treaty with kings and ministers. And there were failures, too, in Abraham's life. But Abraham's entire journey from the first *lekh lekha* to the second was a journey with an awareness of the command, "Walk before Me and be upright" (*Bereishit* 17:1). And God concluded two covenants with Abraham, which are in reality but one: the "Covenant between the Pieces," which is a mighty vision, and the *Brit Mila*, which is a tangible symbol.

But one must not forget that a covenant is a two-sided or two-directional matter, and its observance is dependent on the faithfulness of each of the two sides to his obligations or promises to the other. We know that the one side remembers the covenant, but for us—the sons of Abraham—the other side—the observance of the covenant is dependent upon us, and we are the ones liable to violate it, even if the faithfulness of the Rememberer of the Covenant is unquestionable. This is an important lesson for those who do not stop speaking of "the claims of the forefathers" which exist eternally. They ignore the fact that the greatest of the *Amora'im* and the rabbis of the Midrash and Aggada—and much later, *Rabbenu Tam* and *Ramban* as well—discuss the question of how long "the claims of the forefathers" lasted, or when they ended. Almost all are of the opinion that these have ended, and all that remains is the covenant, which implies no claim but an obligation—to observe the covenant. These Sages were already preceded by *Tanna'im* who stated: "Three things were given conditionally—the Land of Israel, the Temple, and the kingship of the House of David." Who keeps—or who will keep—the conditions of the covenant?

VAYERA

Vayera is the continuation of *Lekh Lekha*, and the two *sidrot* are a single unit—the main points of Abraham's life, and I stress the word "main," for the Torah has not come to tell us the biography of the man named Abraham. The unit which we are discussing does not begin with the childhood and youth of Abraham, which are only mentioned in the most cursory fashion—and that already at the end of the *sidra* of *Noach*. Nor does this unit deal with Abraham's last days—the story of Abraham's old age and his death are left for the *sidra* of *Chayye Sarah*. The unit of *Lekh Lekha-Vayera* is the account of Abraham's journey in *emuna*—faith, of his "walking before God," and both the beginning and end of this journey are marked by the words *lekh lekha*; on the one hand "to the land which I will show you," which would be the home of his descendants; and on the other hand—"to the land of Moria," which was meant to be the place of the *Akeida*, the purpose of his dedication to the service of God.

In my previous talk, I discussed what appears to us as two different degrees of *emuna*: that of believing in God as a result of the promise, "I will protect you," and as opposed to this, the conduct of Abraham at the *Akeida*, where he is granted the title "one who fears God." The first stand of Abram (he is still Abram!) in faith can be interpreted as his being conscious of God's relation to him; the second expresses his being conscious of his relation to God, and the difference between the two is that which was later defined in Jewish religious thought as the difference between "*shelo lishma*"—"not for its own sake"—and "*lishma*"—"for its own sake." (From the mishnaic period on, there is a differentiation made between studying the Torah "for its own sake"—as an end in itself—and studying it "not for its own sake"—as a means for some other purpose. Expanding on this, one must differentiate between worship of God as an end in itself, or worshipping Him as a means for satisfying some human need or want.)

We should also note the fact that the term "fear of God" appears twice in our *sidra*. When he stood before Avimelekh, king of Gerar, Abraham told him, "I thought, surely there is no fear of God in this place; and they will kill me" (*Bereishit* 20:11). Here, the term "fear of God" apparently refers to a type of relationship with a Supreme police force, whose supervision of mankind is an essential condition for people to be able to live together, so that one will not arise against another to swallow him up, in accordance with a later *Tanna*, who lived about 2,000 years later, regarding the necessity for "the fear of the government." From this point of view, fear of God appears as something instrumental, something which is needed for the preservation of society and the protection of mankind, or, in short, to serve man's needs. Lest the reader of the Torah conclude that that was Abraham's fear of God, we have the chapter of the *Akeida*, in which this term appears again, but this time in God's words to Abraham, "Now I know that you fear God" (*Bereishit* 12:12). Again the same phrase—fear of God—but this time, it is not the fear of God regarding which Abraham spoke to Avimelekh, but the exact opposite of it. Here Abraham is not speaking with a gentile king, to whom one must explain the meaning of the fear of God in concepts which he understands. Here, before us, is a man who stands before his God, whom he fears without any regard to the questions of reward and punishment. Thus here, the concept of fear of God blends into that of the love of God. Thus, on the verse, "You shall love God with all your heart and with all your soul and with all your might" (*Devarim* 6:5), R. Akiva said, "Even if He takes your soul" (i.e., "your life"). Indeed, the command, "Take now your son, your only son Isaac....," was as if God had taken Abraham's soul—and not only in terms of the relationship of the father to his only son whom he loved, but also in terms of the annulling of specific Divine promises that had been made to him, something which one would have imagined should have undermined his faith in God. The Midrash points out that Abraham could have offered an extremely strong argument: "Yesterday You told me, 'In Isaac shall your seed be called' (*Bereishit* 21:12), and today You say to me, 'offer him there for a burnt offering' (22:2)." Even further: from the case of Sodom and Gomorra, we see that Abraham was able to argue with God, and had no fear doing so (*Bereishit* 18:25—"Far be it from you...."). But just here, where this affects the depths of his spiritual existence, he remains silent. The Midrash regards this silence as the highest level of faith which Abraham attained. And we understand the difference between the debate over Sodom and the *Akeida*: in the case of Sodom, the topic at hand was justice ("Shall not the Judge of the earth do right?"), which can be understood within the categories of human thought and can be a topic for moral analysis, even with God. And it is not only Abraham who dares to argue with God, for even Avimelekh, king of Gerar, does so ("Will You also slay a righteous nation?"—*Bereishit* 20:4). Here though, when Abraham is commanded, "Take now your son, your only son Isaac....," it is a question of the perfection of faith—and Abraham does not debate that issue. He remains silent, rises early in the morning, saddles his ass, and goes on his way.

Regarding the saddling of the ass (*chamor* in Hebrew), Abarbanel says something extraordinary: "He overcame the physical (*chomriut*) within himself"—the spirituality of his faith overcame the power of human nature. And we are reminded that the very first paragraph in the *Shulchan Arukh*, which imposes on man the obligation to get up to serve God, makes this conditional on, "one shall make a supreme effort."

CHAYYE SARAH

Chayye Sarah is the story of Abraham's last days, his death and his burial. His last days begin with the death of his wife. Only after his wife has died and been buried are we told that, "Abraham was old, and well advanced in age" (*Bereishit* 24:1). The Midrash asks justly: Wasn't Abraham old before this? After all, according to the chronology implied within the narrative about the forefathers, even though it does not say so specifically, Abraham was already old and advanced in age before Sarah died. Rather, the Midrash is telling us a profound psychological truth—that "a man's death hits only his wife, and a woman's death hits only her husband"—that no loss affects a person as greatly as the loss of a spouse. Thus, from the time that Sarah died, old age pounced upon Abraham.

The majority of the *sidra* of *Chayye Sarah* deals with two topics: the acquisition of the cave of Machpela for the burial of Sarah and the long account, which goes into the greatest of detail, of the match of Isaac and Rebecca. Here, though, I would like to discuss the end of the *sidra*, after Sarah had died and been buried, after the widower Abraham had taken care of finding a spouse for his son Isaac, and after Rebecca had arrived and married Isaac. One would have imagined that at that point, Abraham's life was over, but now we are told that he took another wife, named Ketura, and she bore him children. Only then did Abraham die, "old and satisfied of days," after which, "his sons Isaac and Ishmael buried him" (*Bereishit* 25:9). Here we stand astonished. The triangle of Abraham-Isaac-Ishmael was a very harsh, tragic and somber one in Abraham's life, and   it   paralleled   the   triangle   of

Abraham-Sarah-Hagar. Both of these events were very painful, and bear witness to the fact that in Abraham's life—his path in faith—as in the life of every person, there were setbacks and failures. There is no doubt that in regard to these two triangles there was an element of failure. This has been discussed by both the earlier and later commentators. There were great leaders of Torah and faith who clearly condemned Sarah's conduct in "afflicting" Hagar. There is no record of condemnation of the banishment of Hagar and Ishmael, for permission to do so was granted by God; but we can see from the Midrash and the Aggada to what extent this incident bothered pious Torah scholars.

I remember from my childhood that I heard from my Bialystok-born mother that when rumors spread in 1890 that the Turkish regime was about to banish from the Jewish settlements in Palestine those Russian Jews who had moved to the country and had not taken Ottoman citizenship, R. Shmuel Mohiliwer, the rabbi of Bialystok, one of the great rabbis of his generation and one of the leaders of the Chibbat Zion movement, cried and said that it was because of, "Drive out this slave-girl and her son" (*Bereishit* 21:10), that it had been decreed that the son of the slave-girl (the Turks—as Muslims—were called Ishmaelites by the Jews) would now cast out the sons of Sarah from our land. Now though, years after Hagar and her son had been banished to the desert of Paran, and Ishmael had settled there and become "an archer," Abraham died, and "his sons Isaac and Ishmael buried him." Again we find Ishmael within his father's domain. The Torah does not tell us anything of what happened between the time that Hagar and Ishmael were banished and when Ishmael returned. The midrashic and aggadic thought, though, fills in the picture. The midrashic and aggadic tales testify as to how much time the thinkers of the Torah and faith, who attempt to derive faith from the Torah, devoted to pondering over this event, in terms of the injustice that was done, and the undoing of this injustice.

There are remarkable stories, for which we do not have enough time, that Abraham, without the knowledge of his wife Sarah, who had her rival, Hagar, sent away, went twice to the desert to visit his banished son, Ishmael, to find out how he was and what had happened to him. The story is very absorbing, and is also linked to the story of Ishmael's wives. What is most interesting is that the Midrash—this is a very late Midrash—attributes to these wives names drawn from the Arabic tradition of Islam. Of the two wives, one is named Issa, the same name as Mohammed's younger wife, while the second is named Fatima, the name of Mohammed's daughter.

But the main point is that the Midrash states that Ketura was none other than Hagar herself, whom Abraham brought back after Sarah—who had been the cause of Hagar's banishment—died. Not only that, but the Midrash tells us something remarkable: the meeting between Isaac and Rebecca, when Rebecca was brought to her future husband, took place at Be'er Lahai Ro'i, and that was the place where Hagar had gone after fleeing from Sarah. What did Isaac have to do with Be'er Lahai Ro'i? The Midrash says that after his mother Sarah died, Isaac went to bring back his stepmother Hagar, who had been banished because of his mother, from there, so as to return her to his father and to rectify the injustice. The aggadic narrative has much to say in praise of Hagar, whom it identifies as Ketura, and it states: "Why was she called Ketura? Because her deeds were as pleasant as incense" (*ketoret* in Hebrew). This figurative interpretation indicates to what extent the great believers of our world studied the actions of our forefathers, paused at every blemish or defect of theirs, and sought to rectify them. From this, there is much for all generations to learn: that one should not idealize everything that has occurred in the past but should see things as they were, should understand them, should judge them, and should consequently think of how to rectify them.

I would like to convey here an aggadic thought of great significance, which deals with the three wives of Abraham: Sarah was of the daughters of Shem, Hagar (the Egyptian) was of Cham, whereas Ketura (which this Midrash does not identify with Hagar) was of

Yafet. This indicates (or gives us a hint) that from Abraham there emanated—or there will yet emanate—enlightenment for all the races of mankind.

TOLDOT

The *sidra* known as *Toldot Yitzchak*, or "the history of Isaac," is not, in reality, a biography of Isaac, but the beginning of the history of his descendants, his children and later his grandchildren—a story which, in terms of its scope, is a major part of the book of Genesis.

The Book of Genesis tells us very little about Isaac. We know nothing of his childhood and youth, except for the great event where he went with his father for the *Akeida*. Only a later Midrash tells us that when Isaac went, it was an act of self-sacrifice on his part as well. What we are told primarily is the story of the birth of his sons, incidents between the sons, and incidents between them and their father.

In terms of Isaac's life, all we hear of is the triangle of Isaac-Rebecca-Avimelekh, which is a kind of repetition of the case of Abraham-Sarah-Avimelekh; and we hear of the wells that he dug. And that happens to be a very interesting point. Isaac, who at first blush seems to be a most passive character, is the only one of our forefathers who attempts to realize the goal of acquiring the land by an actual attempt at settling it. Abraham and Jacob were both nomads. Only Isaac—who, we are told, sowed and watered the soil—obtained crops from the ground. As mentioned, though, immediately after these events, we find Isaac as an old man who has, for all practical purposes, forsaken an active life, is half-blind and stays at home, while events run their course without any cooperation on his part.

As opposed to this, the story of Jacob, which begins in the same *sidra*, is, in terms of scope, the major portion of the Book of

Genesis, and it evokes a human image that we learn to know in all its detail. Jacob's character emerges from the book with great clarity, in a much more alive and colorful form than not only Isaac, but even Abraham, of whose childhood and youth we know nothing. For example, we know absolutely nothing about Abraham's mother, and only a very late Midrash gives her a strange name, which has no basis in the Torah text.

On the other hand, regarding Jacob, we know of his conception and birth, of his childhood and youth. This is the full account of a person's life, with its struggles, achievements, failures and successes. I think I will not be erring when I state that, historically, Jacob's life, as told in Genesis, is the first personal biography of which we are aware in world literature. The portrayal of Jacob is the most human of the forefathers. It is true that he too was among those who "walked before God," but this walking was embodied in a life which included human suffering and pain, and included tests which the average person also undergoes, and which are understandable to us, the common people, more than the tests to which Abraham was subjected when he stood before God.

Jacob's life story includes jealousy and competition, issues between the sexes, struggles over acquisition and property, the pain of raising children, failures and victories. Jacob himself, in his old age, said that, "the days of my life were few and hard when compared to the lives of my ancestors" (*Bereishit* 47:9), and this is discussed by the later *midrashim*. *Tanchuma* says: "He suffered greatly." A very late Midrash has God saying about Jacob: "I never performed any miracles for him." On our part, we can say that all of Jacob's life was but a series of hidden miracles, but there were indeed no open miracles in his life. Jacob's character was both complex and enigmatic. On the one hand, he was "blameless," the first term applied to him. At the same time, he was clever and cunning, and sometimes even sly. It was he, as he dwelled in tents and was guided by his mother, who was revealed later as a practical man and as one of achievements, whose wife was not brought to him from the outside. He acquired his wives and his possessions by his own efforts, work and acumen. It was because of his love for a woman that he dedicated himself to work in which he engaged for many years. He, who on the one hand appeared to be afraid of his brother and to act obsequiously before him, was the same person who "contended with God and with men." Not only that, but close to his death we hear directly from his mouth, to our great surprise, that in Cana'an he conquered a certain area with his sword and bow, something of which we are given no earlier indication.

Whatever he was supposed to receive, he obtained in a round-about and complex way. It was clear from the outset that he was meant to be the spiritual heir to Abraham, but he achieved this by questionable and circuitous means. The birthright and the blessing which were meant for him, the wife who was meant for him, his wealth and his acquisitions—none of these were given to him via the straight path—but he was forced to acquire them through difficult struggles, by overcoming obstacles, and meeting with failures. Yet, at the same time, he was granted a great prophetic vision, and afterwards God appeared to him another three times, and directed his life. Finally it was this man, Jacob, who "deceived his brother" (a Hebrew pun on the name Jacob—*Hoshea* 12:4), who became Israel, who contended with God and men. It is not for naught that our nation is called by his name, for our history in many ways parallels the life of our father Jacob.

VAYETZE

"Jacob went out" (*Bereishit* 28:10). With what did Jacob leave his father's house to go into exile? He left with the birthright and the blessing which he had acquired by roundabout means, means which were a mixture of the positive and the negative. But beyond these, which included the great mission which had devolved upon him from Abraham, he had nothing. As he himself would testify twenty years later regarding the dramatic episodes in which he was involved when he obtained the birthright and the blessing, he had crossed the Jordan with nothing more than his staff. The first great event after he left his home was the prophetic vision that he saw. That dream has revealed profound allusions, hidden meanings and significant messages to generation after generation of those who studied the Torah, those who interpreted it, and those who offered homiletic messages based upon it. After this dream, after he awoke from his sleep, Jacob took a vow. That vow is surprising for a number of reasons, and I would like to devote the few minutes available to us to this small episode of Jacob's vow.

This vow is surprising, first of all, in the fact that after Jacob was granted this revelation of God, which included the promise of a glorious future, he spoke, as it were, only of satisfying his material needs: bread to eat and clothing to wear. More than that, it seems as if he made a condition: if his wants were granted and God aided him—so one may understand it—then God would be his God.

But one can explain this in an entirely different way, and that was also the way it was understood by those who learned the book of Genesis throughout the generations. Jacob did not impose any condition here on the acceptance of the Yoke of the Kingdom of Heaven. "God will be my God" (*Bereishit* 28:21) was not a *quid pro quo* which Jacob promised, but was included in those things he sought: bread to eat, clothes to wear, to return to his father's house, and that God should be his God. But the Midrash delves into this more deeply, and converts Jacob's vow from a request that he made for the supplying of his needs to an obligation which he accepted upon himself *vis-à-vis* God. Let us reproduce the words of the Midrash:

> "If God is with me and protects me on the path on which I am going" (*Bereishit* 28:20)—"on the path (in Hebrew, "*baderekh*")"—that he will preserve me from *lashon hara* (slander), in accordance with the verse, "They bend (*vayidrekhu*) their tongues like their bow for lies;" "and He will give me bread to eat" (*Yirmiyahu* 9:2)—He will preserve me from lewdness, in accordance with the well-known allusion to "the bread I eat" as referring to sexual relations; "and I return in peace to my father's house"—to be taken literally: to refrain from spilling blood; "and God will be my God": He will preserve me from idolatry.

This means that Jacob was not seeking to have his needs taken care of, but wanted God to help him fulfill his obligations, by preventing him from committing slander, murder, lewdness and idolatry. This vow was not a request for a reward, but a great religious commitment.

But the midrashic literature delves even more deeply into this matter, in an almost frightening way. The Midrash notes that Jacob regressed to such a state that, based on the literal meaning of the text, he begged for bread to eat and clothes to wear, because he had absolutely nothing: he had crossed the Jordan with his staff, and he begged to be able to return in peace, because he was in great distress and great danger. But what caused him to reach that state? The fact that he had obtained the birthright and the blessing by devious ways, and as a result earned the enmity of his brother, Esau; it was because of this that he had been forced to flee and to go into exile. The Midrash does not show any partiality toward Jacob, and makes the following shocking statement:

> All those things which Jacob wished to refrain from, came upon him. He wished to refrain from slander, and what happened to him and his household? "Joseph brought to his father their evil report" (*Bereishit* 37:2). Jacob wished to refrain from lewdness, and in his household, the events of Reuben and Bilha, and of Judah and Tamar took place. He very much wished to live in peace and to refrain from shedding blood, and the affair of Shekhem and Simeon and Levi occurred—an action for which one can find justification ("Should he deal with our sister as with a harlot?"—*Bereishit* 34:31), but which was nevertheless an action whose accursedness Jacob mentioned decades later, just before he died. Whatever Jacob wished to refrain from occurred to him: slander, lewdness in his family, the shedding of blood, and even idolatry—Rachel took her father's idols into Jacob's home, and later Jacob had to demand the removal of the foreign gods "in their midst."

Here we see that God does not show partiality even to His chosen ones. On the contrary: one may even say that it is specifically to His chosen ones that he does *not* show partiality. That is why the Chosen One of the forefathers (as Jacob is commonly known), who attained the heavenly mission assigned to him, underwent all these terrible events. He suffered all these failures because, on his way to attain his mission, he did not follow the straight path.

VAYISHLACH

The meeting between Jacob and Esau, after a separation which lasted twenty years, raises many problems: Jacob arrives at this meeting after having obtained a Divine promise that he will return in peace to his father's house. Even more than that: just before this meeting he meets messengers of God who have come to greet him as he returns to Cana'an, and to escort him along the way. Yet, after all of this, Jacob sends messengers to Esau to show his obsequiousness to his brother, and to beg for his life and that of his family. How can we understand this? Did Jacob lack faith in the Divine promise? Or was he by nature fainthearted, so that he was afraid in spite of that promise? Yet the Torah tells us that the night before this meeting, Jacob struggled "with God and with men" (*Bereishit* 32:29). He remained alone at night, without any cover or defense, and was attacked by someone who, according to one midrashic interpretation, appeared to him as an armed robber, or, according to another interpretation, appeared to him from the very first moment as a celestial being. But regardless of how his assailant appeared to him, Jacob was faced by someone terrible and frightening, with whom he struggled the entire night. And indeed, afterwards the Torah says about Jacob, "You strove with God and with men" (*Bereishit* 32:21), implying extraordinary courage. Why then was Jacob suddenly so obsequious before his brother?

The answer is a clear one: Jacob was not a fearful person, and was not afraid of the dangers that might lie in store for him and his family by any outside force, but he was terribly afraid of his own self-accusation. He knew that he had sinned against his brother

twenty years earlier, and he did not have the courage to fight his
brother with the same strength that he had shown in striving even
with an angel, for he did not have a clear conscience in regard to
Esau. He was willing to humiliate himself before his brother, if only
that would prevent him from having to fight the brother against
whom he had committed a wrong for which he now had to atone.
This is not some kind of arbitrary interpretation about Jacob's
psychology, but can be proven from the text itself. At the beginning,
there are a number of references made to the gift that Jacob sent to
Esau, and when the two meet, Jacob speaks of "my gift" (*Bereishit*
33:10). Afterwards, as they continue talking, when it becomes clear
that both have been reconciled and that Esau does not intend to harm
him, Jacob exclaims, "Take my blessing that I have brought you"
(*Bereishit* 33:11). This is a strange slip of the tongue: rather than
speaking of a "gift," Jacob uses the word, "blessing." One may say
that this is a Freudian slip: Jacob remembers the whole story of the
blessing that he stole from Esau, and therefore now, when they have
made peace with one another, he characterizes this reconciliation as
a form of a return of the blessing to his brother.

That same night, before the fateful meeting, Jacob engages in the
tremendous struggle, which will later be referred to as "striving with
God and with men," and which results in his name being changed.
The name Jacob, which in Hebrew has overtones of crooked and
warped elements within the human condition, is now changed to
Israel. It is like a transformation in Jacob's life: from being Jacob to
becoming a man of God, Israel. One should note that this was
known to all of the later generations. At least a thousand years later,
after the affair of Jacob and Esau, the prophet Hosea tells us: "He
took his brother by the heel (*akev* in Hebrew) in the womb" (a pun
on "he deceived him") (*Hoshea* 12:4). In other words, the Jewish
people retained within their national awareness the knowledge that
Jacob had done something unseemly. More than a hundred years
after Hosea, the prophet of the destruction, Jeremiah, in rebuking the
people of his generation for their lies, hypocrisy and deceit, uses the

phrase, "for every brother will utterly deceive" (in Hebrew, *akov ya'akov*) (*Yirmiyahu* 9:3). At first glance, it appears that there is no reference to Jacob, for Jeremiah is speaking to his contemporaries, but he indicates their dishonesty by reminding them of the brother Jacob—in Hebrew Ya'akov—who deceived his brother.

This journey, the journey from Jacob to Israel, is the journey, which was laid out for the Jewish people, and we are still not sure if it will reach its planned destination.

In regard to this, we have to discuss the story of Shekhem, a major event in Jacob's life, and, to be more accurate, in the life of Jacob's sons, from whom the Jewish people arose. This act of Shekhem certainly had a justification for, "Should he deal with our sister as with a harlot?" (*Bereishit* 34:31). These are the last words uttered about the event. Nevertheless, decades later, when Jacob was on his deathbed and was offering indications as to his sons' future, he cursed two of his sons, two of the progenitors of the tribes of Israel. Even though that deed seemed to have justification, it became a curse for the future. If we say that "the histories of the fathers are a paradigm for their children," that is what can be said about the achievements of the Jewish people when they are achieved through flawed and improper means, and, worst of all—through bloodshed. About 800 years after Jacob, David too recognized—and admitted twice—that "as a man of war" who had "spilled much blood," he too was not fitting, and was not even permitted, to build the Temple (I *Divrei Hayamim* 22:8; 28:3).

VAYESHEV

The three *sidrot* of *Vayeshev*, *Miketz* and *Vayigash* contain the unparalleled dramatic story of the events occurring in the lives of Jacob and his household until our forefathers went down to Egypt. This time, though, I have chosen not to speak about the story itself, but about a midrashic comment on the story, in order to present, by means of an allusion—but a very transparent one—one of the greatest, most keen and profound problems in human thought, both in the field of religious-theological thinking and in the field of anthropological-philosophical thinking.

We are referring to a passage in *Midrash Tanchuma* on the present *sidra*, which comments on the words, "Joseph was brought down to Egypt" (*Bereishit* 39:1). This is what the Midrash has to say: "This is as is seen in the verse, 'Come and see the works of God: He is terrible in His dealing (עלילה) with men' (*Tehillim* 66:5)." The latter is a verse in Psalms which, according to its simple meaning, does not arouse any doubts: it expresses the greatness of God's deeds in the world. But the Midrash latches onto the dual meaning of the word עלילה. The word means "deeds," but it also has the meaning of a false accusation levelled against another person. Here the Midrash dares to use the latter meaning in reference to God.

R. Joshua b. Karhah said: "Even those events which You bring upon us, You bring with עלילה." In other words, God brings about deeds in the world and upon man, and then later places the blame on man. The Midrash then goes on to bring three examples of this from the Torah, one of which we will bring in the actual language of the

Midrash, whereas the others will merely be mentioned. Before God created the world, He created the Angel of Death on the first day. How do we know this? R. Perahiah said: "It is because it states, 'there was darkness upon the face of the deep' [it is at this point that creation began]. That is a reference to the Angel of Death, who darkens the face of all creatures. Man was created on the sixth day, and an עלילה was placed against him, that it was he that brought death upon the world." The Angel of Death was created before man was created. In other words, from the outset it was determined that man would be mortal. Yet according to the story of Adam and Eve, it was because of them that death was decreed upon mankind.

"To what is this analogous?" The analogy is a marvelous one: "to a man who wished to divorce his wife. When he wanted to enter his house, he wrote a *get* (a divorce document) and entered the house with the *get* in his pocket. He then sought an עלילה to give it to her. He told her, 'Pour me a cup that I may drink.' She poured it for him. As soon as he took the cup, he said to her, 'This is your *get*.' She said to him: 'What did I do wrong?' He said: 'Go out of my house, because you poured for me a lukewarm cup.' She said to him, 'Did you already know that I would pour for you a lukewarm cup, that you wrote the *get* and brought it in your hand?' So too did Adam say to God"—in reality, Adam did not say it, but the Midrash wishes to say that Adam could have said to God: "Lord of the Universe! Two thousand years before You created Your world, You wrote in the Torah, 'If a man should die in the tent' [according to the Midrash, the Torah preceded the creation of the world by 2,000 years]. If that is so, about 2,000 years before You created the world, You wrote in the Torah about a man dying. Are you now coming to accuse me of bringing about death?" In the same vein, the Midrash tells of it having been decreed a considerable time before the waters of Meriva that Moses would die—and the Midrash proves this from the Torah text—yet later the Torah blames this on Moses' sin.

All of these matters are a prologue to the story of Joseph, the third example brought by the Midrash. Two generations before the events told in *Vayeshev*, Abraham, Jacob's grandfather, was told, "Know this for certain that your descendants will be aliens in a land that is not theirs, and will be slaves and oppressed four hundred years" (*Bereishit* 15:13). Now God brought about the entire affair of Jacob and his sons, the competition and the hatred between the other brothers and Joseph, the sale of Joseph, his elevation to high office in Egypt, and the bringing down of Jacob and his sons to that land, in order to fulfill what He had said earlier. Why should the brothers be to blame for having caused the family to go down to Egypt? After all, this had been decided in advance. Therefore, "it is an עלילה toward men."

What is the meaning of this Midrash? It hints at one of the greatest, most keen and profound problems in human thought, going back to ancient times—from the earliest days of human thought—to the present, both in the realm of faith and in the realm of philosophy, which does not recognize religious faith at all. Both are faced with the same problem, which, in the philosophical formulation, is labelled the problem of determinism and free will.

In the realm of faith, this is the conflict between the notion of Divine providence, which directs man's actions and determines the future ("all is foreseen" by God). As opposed to this, we have the concept of free will, which places upon man the responsibility for those actions he takes of his own will. In the realm of general philosophy, the same problem exists. Even if the concept of "Divine Providence" does not exist at all, there is the concept of causality, which is a sort of objective providence without the existence of a subject which orders matters: embedded within the nature of the cosmic reality is causality—everything is due to what preceded it and is the cause of what follows it. According to this, one might venture to claim that there is no free will. But in terms of man's intuitive recognition, he cannot refrain from the expression that he is acting of his own will.

Innumerable attempts have been made to solve this problem, which is among that class of issues which, in the philosophical terminology, are known as antinomies and paralogisms. In the realm of faith, there is sometimes the tendency to postulate predestination, which annuls man's free will, and it is possible that this Midrash is referring to exactly that. On another plane of profound religious thought, the concept of providence is explained in an entirely different fashion: not as having man's actions and fate decreed from above, but as man's ascent from below to comprehending God. In this I am but hinting at the solution of Maimonides, who maintains the principle of the free will of man, who only by his own endeavors gains Divine providence for himself—but this is not the place to dwell at length on this great issue. Similarly, in the area of philosophical recognition, there are those who cast doubts about determinism: Is the world run according to strict causality, or are there within nature itself events which are not the result of a previous cause? And even if we do admit that there is causality in nature, is human consciousness itself part of the natural reality subject to causality, or does it have freedom which does not exist in nature? These problems are hinted at in the midrashic interpretation of the three Hebrew words in our *sidra*: "Joseph was brought down to Egypt."

MIKETZ

"Two years later, Pharaoh had a dream" (*Bereishit* 41:1). This is one of the many dreams in Genesis, which, in many ways, is different from the other *chumashim*. One of the unique aspects of the book is its being the world of dreams. In the other books of the Bible, on the other hand, dreams do not play an important part. The prophets generally belittle dreams, and Zekharia tells us, "dreams speak falsehood" (*Zekharia* 10:2). Only when we come to the period of the Second Temple and Daniel, do we again enter the world of dreams.

The dreams contained in Genesis are extremely significant: they either depict the future, or are the cause of events which take place later as a result of these dreams.

Everyone dreams in Genesis: the forefathers: Abraham sees the Covenant of the Pieces (*Bereishit* 15) after a deep sleep falls upon him; Jacob, who dreams the great dream of the ladder; and Joseph, who is known as "the dreamer." But even Avimelekh, king of Gerar, has God appear to him in a dream, and the same is true for Laban the Aramean. Even two Egyptian servants of Pharaoh, who had been removed from their posts and were imprisoned, dream very significant dreams; but the idea of the significant dream ends with the conclusion of Genesis.

One could begin a very profound discussion here: Why is it that the world before the giving of the Torah was a world permeated with significant dreams, whereas from the giving of the Torah onwards, dreams lost their significance? I will limit myself to this allusion, and would like to discuss two great dreams in Genesis: the dreams of two people who—whether we relate to them historically or whether we relate to them symbolically—represent the two extremes of humanity.

On the one hand, we have Jacob, the Chosen One of the forefathers, the "blameless" man; and on the other hand, Pharaoh, the king of Egypt. Pharaoh here possibly does not refer to the historical Pharaoh, but to the symbolic Pharaoh—who was many generations later dubbed by the prophet Ezekiel as "the great dragon that lies in the midst of his rivers" (*Yechezkel* 29:3). Jacob represents the Divine in man, while Pharaoh represents the animal in him—yet both have dreams. In regard to both of these dreams, the Midrash makes a very profound statement, which displays the two different aspects of the world of faith, possibly of all religious faith, of the perception of man's status before God.

In all generations of human history, a religious belief has prevailed, a belief in gods—who are not God. There is deep significance, historical and/or symbolical, in the fact that Genesis portrays a reality where there is no person who does not know God, whether he engages in idolatry or not. Not only our forefathers believe in Him, but even before them there are righteous men that "walk with God." In Abraham's time, too, there lived in Cana'an Malkhizedek, king of Salem, and Avimelekh, king of Gerar. In Aram, there were Bethuel and Laban (notwithstanding their household "images"). The same was even true for Pharaoh, king of Egypt—they all knew God. In the world of Genesis, there is no person who denies God—not even the wicked generations of the flood and of the Tower of Babel.

What then is unique in the faith of Abraham, Isaac and Jacob? The Midrash of the dreams attempts to answer the question.

Pharaoh dreams, "he was standing by the river"—the river, of course, was the Nile. "Standing by the river" means at the river bank. But if we take the Hebrew literally, Pharaoh was standing *on* (על) the river. What was the significance of the Nile to the Egyptians? To them, the Nile was Egypt. Egypt exists only because of the river and due to its power. Had there not been this river, which cuts across Egypt from south to north, Egypt would have been nothing but a continuation of the desert to its west, of the great Libyan desert, which has no rainfall whatsoever; and it is only because of this great river that a thin strip, measuring but a few miles in width, of fertile land was made available, thus permitting human habitation. And not only that, but it permits the greatest population density in the world.

The area which the Nile irrigates is not greater than the area of the Land of Israel. All the rest is a vast desert where not even a blade of grass grows; and it is in this thin strip that 50 million people live today; and that is how it has been for as far back as we can go. Egypt was created by the Nile, and its existence depends on the Nile. Mythologically, the river is the god of Egypt, through which Egypt exists. The Egyptians would worship the Nile, and it was their god. It is to this that the Midrash alludes when it states on the verse, "'Pharaoh dreamed that he was standing on the river'—the wicked maintain themselves on their gods, but the righteous—God stands on them, as it states (in regard to Jacob), 'He dreamed that a ladder set up on earth, and its top reached to heaven: and angels of God ascending and descending on it (*alav* in Hebrew). And God stood on it' (*Bereishit* 28:12–13)." In Hebrew, the word "*alav*" may mean either "on it" or "on him;" therefore, according to the meaning of the text, God stood above the ladder, but taken literally, God stood on Jacob.

What is the meaning of this profound Midrash? In both cases, we have people who were aware of man's status before God—both men had faith. Pharaoh, too, who worshipped idolatry, was a man of faith, but he regarded his god as a means to supply his needs. His god existed for him. He had a god that carried him; a god for his needs, to do good for him and to enable him to survive. But Jacob accepted upon himself to carry his God; he did not demand that God should keep him alive, but accepted upon himself to keep his faith in God. Jacob's God is not a tool for human interests; Jacob sees man, and consequently the entire world, as tools for the maintenance of the worship of God.

This is the difference between true religious faith and between idolatrous faith, or—in the language of our Sages—between "for its own sake" and "not for its own sake," between the Chosen One of the forefathers who dreamed and Pharaoh, king of Egypt, who also dreamed.

VAYIGASH

"Then Judah came near to him" (*Bereishit* 44:18). The meeting between Judah and Joseph, and the dialogue that followed it, marks one of the most dramatic incidents in the striking narrative of the children of Jacob, the forefathers of the tribes of Israel, until their exile into Egypt. The confrontation between them appears as a model of a later midrashic and interpretational rule—"the histories of the fathers are a paradigm for the children." Hundreds of years before the historic events, we have an instance of the confrontation between the tribe of Judah and what would later be known as Israel, the ten tribes led by the tribe of Ephraim, Joseph's son. It is this symbolic significance which led to the choice of the *haftara* being the vision of Ezekiel, which speaks of the reunification of the kingdoms of Judah and of the house of Joseph.

It appears that the tribe of Judah on the one hand, and the ten tribes on the other, never really merged into a single state. Even during the days of David and Solomon, they appear to have been two separate kingdoms under a joint king who ruled both. And immediately after Solomon came the partition, a decisive event in the history of Israel; and one of the most active in this partition was the prophet Achiah the Shilonite. It was that division which determined the historical course of the Israelite nation, which was later known as the Jewish people of our day, because all that remained of that nation was the tribe of Judah (hence "Jewish"), whose descendants we all are.

The vast majority of the Israelite people were lost as a result of this decisive partition. This was the part of the people from which the prophet Elijah—who to this day is considered to be the messenger who visits each *brit mila*—arose, but he did not manage to instill a covenant (*brit*) between the ten tribes and Judah. The prophets Amos and Hosea, who very possibly never set foot in Judah, and who may never have been in Jerusalem, also arose among the ten tribes.

The *haftara* of this *sidra* is evidently a prophecy for the future: the unification of Judah and Joseph and the political and spiritual rehabilitation of the united nation after it had become two separate nations. This prophecy has not been fulfilled.

It thus follows that we should study and deliberate on the significance of the prophecies related to the future, of what appear to be statements by the prophets as to what will occur. Ezekiel prophesied after both the ten tribes and Judah had already been exiled. His contemporary, Jeremiah, who began prophesying while the kingdom of Judah still existed, but more than a hundred years after the exile of the ten tribes, foretold in a very emotional style and in an effusive manner, the return of the ten tribes. This particular prophecy became very popular, referring as it does to Rachel weeping for her children Ephraim and Menashe, and God's promise to her that they would return. So too do we have, "Is Ephraim my dear son? Is he a child of my delight?…. I will yet remember him" (*Yirmiyahu* 31:20). Hosea and Amos too, who foretold the destruction of the kingdom of Israel, added that in the future Israel will return. This did not occur. And in this case, it is also impossible to accept the midrashic view of prophecies that have not been fulfilled to this day—that these are prophecies for the End of Days and will yet be fulfilled. The ten tribes, including the descendants of Joseph, were destroyed off the face of the earth; they were evidently not destroyed physically, but were destroyed spiritually; they were totally assimilated among the nations to which they had been exiled, and there is no trace of them historically since that time. Already in talmudic times, R. Akiva, who, like us, was aware of the prophecies of the return of the ten tribes, stated that "the ten tribes will not return." He knew that they were lost.

This in no way undermined R. Akiva's faith in "the prophets of truth and justice," because he understood that their words were not foretelling what would happen, but were rather a presentation of what ought to occur, and why it is proper that it should occur, and are a goal for which we should hope and strive, even though there is no guarantee that it will take place. More than 1,500 years after Ezekiel and Jeremiah, and more than 1,000 years after R. Akiva, we are told in *Tosafot*: "No prophet foretells but what ought to occur, if there is no sin." The false prophets throughout the generations preach the importance of faith in the certainty of a redemption which is not conditional on anything; of redemption—even if man does not redeem himself from sin.

VAYECHI

The *sidra* of *Vayechi* is the story of Jacob's death, and the *haftara* which is read relates to David's death. In this chapter of the Torah and that chapter of the Prophets, two of the great figures of the Bible die, great both in the religious and historical consciousness of the Jewish people—the Chosen of the Forefathers and "the Anointed of the God of Jacob." Before they die, both command their sons. Jacob transfers to his sons the blessing of Abraham and the great mission of walking before God, as he and his father before him did; and adds a severe note of censure to those of his sons who did not follow the proper path. David bequeaths to his son Solomon the covenant of the kingship, but the main thing he commands him to do may be referred to in modern parlance as the "settling of accounts." It is worth discussing the vast difference between the two.

The two great figures of Jacob and David have certain similarities in their lives: each has a remarkable life, a convoluted one filled with struggles, both externally and internally; struggles with enemies and struggles with his own passions; both have glorious victories in both the physical and spiritual sense, as well as significant failures in the spiritual and moral sense. But at the end of his days, Jacob is elevated to the level of one who sees the End of Days, and notes the great goal of walking in the way of God for the generations that will come after him. David's image has two facets: in his life, too, there are numerous achievements and victories, as well as failures. He battles outside enemies and defeats them, but he also contends with himself and becomes the image of the penitent, who, when the prophet brings to his attention the sin which he has committed, does not attempt to apologize, to justify himself, or to evade the issue. Rather, he says the words, "I have sinned to God." That is why he is remembered in our Jewish consciousness as one who repented and as the person to whom the book of Psalms may be attributed. On the other hand, he is the same king who, before his death, commands his heir to kill two people whom he regards as posing a danger to the king's status: one a man who cursed him in his life, and whom he did not punish; and the second one who was his trusty general, who fought his battles, who shed blood for him, and the one primarily through whom David achieved what he did. At the end of David's days, though, he followed Adonia, one of David's other sons, rather than following Solomon, and therefore, in order to strengthen Solomon in his reign, David commands Solomon to have Joab killed.

Who is the true David? "Ruling over men in justice, ruling in the fear of God" (II *Shmuel* 23:3)—was that David? Or was he a tyrant who "settled accounts" in order to strengthen the monarchy? Actually, David had elements of both. There is a contradiction between the image of David as the great penitent and as the one who carries out the functions of the king, or, in other words—one who is guided by state interests. Our Sages have already told us in this regard: "Woe to the lordship, for it buries those who hold it." Lordship buries those who hold it, meaning that it corrupts a person. There is also a famous saying by one of the leading modern historians (Lord Acton): "Power tends to corrupt; absolute power corrupts absolutely." So too did our Sages say: "No person becomes a leader (*Rosh* in Hebrew) below unless he has become a villain (*Rasha*) above." The Anointed of the God of Jacob, too, who is deemed to be a righteous and Godfearing ruler, necessarily becomes a tyrant and villain by the very fact that he is a king.

This must be repeated to those who regard the sovereignty in Israel as the realization of the most lofty faith and moral goals. Sovereignty is a lofty and precious value for Israel, for it means that the Jewish people will not be subject to other nations. But elevating the power contained within statehood to a supreme value is a very major source of harm. Proof of this can be seen in the comparison between Jacob, who had no governmental power or force, but who at the end of his life foretold the End of Days; and King David, who had the backing of governmental power and force, but who, at the end of his days, was revealed as a man whose political interests shunted aside all his great goals. This is a great lesson for all generations, including ours.

CHUMASH

SHEMOT

SHEMOT

At the Covenant between the Pieces, Abraham was told, "Know for certain that your descendants will be aliens in a land that is not theirs, and will be slaves; and will be oppressed four hundred years" (*Bereishit* 15:13). After these four hundred years, we are told in our *sidra*, "God looked upon the Israelites, and God knew" (*Shemot* 2:25). "God knew" corresponds to "know for certain."

The bondage of Egypt, Moses' birth and his youth, his fleeing to Midian, God's revealing Himself in the burning bush, Moses' mission to Pharaoh, his standing together with his brother Aaron before Pharaoh, the first spark of the redemption from Egyptian bondage—all of these are to be found in this *sidra*.

Here I would like to examine three great words in Hebrew, among the loftiest in the Torah, which, throughout all generations, have been a starting point for theological and philosophical thought on faith—the words אהיה אשר אהיה *EHEYEH ASHER EHEYEH* (which have been variously rendered in English as "I am that I am;" "I am, that is who I am;" "I will be what I will be;" and many other interpretive formulations), and the two verses which follow it.

Moses asks, "When I will say to the Israelites, 'The God of your fathers has sent me to you;' and they will ask me, 'What is his name?' what will I say to them?" (*Shemot* 3:13). His question is how one can know God, and the answer is, "*EHEYEH ASHER EHEYEH*."

There have been innumerable explanations of these great words, and innumerable ideas and meanings have been attached to them, with different, and even contradictory, interpretations. It is, in any

event, clear that these words are related to the root היה, namely, that
they relate to being. "*EHEYEH ASHER EHEYEH*"—true Being,
which is the very essence of the Godhead. In the words of Maimonides: "He is the true Being," and Moses grasped "the truth of
His being." But immediately afterwards, Moses is told, "Thus will
you say to the Israelites, '*EHEYEH* has sent me to you.'" Moreover,
God said to Moses, "Thus will you say to the Israelites, 'The Lord
God of your forefathers, the God of Abraham, the God of Isaac, and
the God of Jacob, has sent me to you: this is My name for ever, and
this is My memorial to all generations.'" Twice Moses is told, "Say
to the Israelites," even though he does not ask any additional question between God's first and second statements. Was he charged to
give two separate answers to the Israelites, or was this all one
answer?

Moses was allowed to recognize God in terms of *EHEYEH
ASHER EHEYEH*, which is a recognition of God in terms of His
Godhead in itself, without any link to the functions which we
attribute to Him. At first, it seems that Moses was told to tell this to
the Israelites, but immediately afterwards he was instructed to give
another answer—because recognizing God in the sense of His
Godhead is something very difficult, and only the strongest believers
can attain this. Most believers are unable to comprehend faith in
God except in terms of their faith in the functions which they
attribute to Him, in terms of their fate and the fate of the nation—
concerning the fact that He is the God of Abraham, Isaac and Jacob.

But one should note that all the depth of the perception of faith
which appears to stem from theological thought is already to be
found in what is customarily regarded as an expression of naive faith
in Judaism. In the *siddur*, among the first blessings of the morning
prayer, we are told: "You are what You are before the world was
created, and You are what You are since the world was created"—
that is a recognition of God without any link to the world, recognition of Him in terms of Himself, in terms of Him being the real
Being. Therefore Moses was told: You may tell them, "*EHEYEH*"

has sent me to you. If they do not understand that, add that "the God of your forefathers, the God of Abraham, the God of Isaac and the God of Jacob has sent me to you." In other words, it is the God that you recognize in terms of what He did for our forefathers, and we hope He will help us as well.

That is the great and fundamental difference between the two planes of the world of faith, both of which are recognized as valid: the recognition of God in terms of His Godhead and the recognition of God in terms of the functions which mortals attribute to Him. And it is from these two that the differentiation between the two approaches in serving God stems, the difference between the two approaches being known, in the language of the Talmud, as "Torah for its own sake" and "Torah not for its own sake." In accordance with this, one can differentiate between service of God "for its own sake" (i.e., as an ultimate end) and service of God "not for its own sake" (i.e., as a means rather than as an end). Service of God for its own sake is where a person serves God because he acknowledges His Godhead; whereas in the case of "not for its own sake," the person serves God because he hopes, or expects or believes, that this service will be beneficial or good for him. Both planes are acceptable, and Maimonides articulates this forcefully and clearly: "The Torah permitted people to serve God and observe the *mitzvot* in the hope of a reward, and to refrain from sinning because of the fear of punishment."

If the Torah permitted this, who am I to forbid it? But the very phrasing, "the Torah permitted," shows us that there is a demand which goes beyond this. It is the recognition of God embodied in the words *EHEYEH ASHER EHEYEH*, that Moses understood, and that those who follow in his footsteps are able to understand. There is also a "God of Abraham, a God of Isaac and a God of Jacob," and that too is a form in which one who believes in God can believe in Him, and this is permitted by the Torah.

Another note. We are told that Moses hid his face, because, "he was afraid to look upon God" (*Shemot* 3:6). Yet this is the same Moses of whom we are told later, "God spoke to Moses face to face" (*Shemot* 33:11) and "the sight of God does he behold" (*Bamidbar* 12:8). There is no contradiction between the two. "The sight of God does he behold"—a true recognition of God—is only the recognition that no man can recognize God. Moses thus "hid his face" because he recognized God.

This is expressed more profoundly by *Rashi*, in which we see the embodiment of naive but complete faith, on the words of the Talmud: "All the prophets looked through a dark glass, and our teacher Moses looked through a clear glass." *Rashi* adds and explains: "All the prophets looked through a dark glass—and thought that they saw Him, and our teacher Moses looked through a clear glass—and knew that he had not seen Him to His face." That is the recognition of the transcendent God.

VA'ERA

"God spoke to Moses, and said to him, 'I am God (the Hebrew uses the tetragrammaton): I appeared to Abraham, to Isaac, and to Jacob, as [or: by the name of] God *Shaddai*, but by My name *THE LORD* (i.e., the tetragrammaton) was I not known to them' (*Shemot* 6:2–3)."

The three great names of God appear in these two verses: the tetragrammaton, the name *Elohim*, and the name *Shaddai*. We do not read the tetragrammaton the way it is written, but rather pronounce it as indicating lordship, and that is the way it appears in the Septuagint translation into Greek, and was later taken over—from the Septuagint (and the Vulgate)—in the translations into modern languages. The word *Elohim* in later Jewish theological thought is "the Mighty and Omnipotent and the Master of all Forces," and the Septuagint translates it by the term the Greeks used for their gods.

But what is *Shaddai*?

According to the verses quoted above, that is the name by which God "was known" to our forefathers, Abraham, Isaac and Jacob. It is true that in the narrative of the forefathers there are references to the tetragrammaton, as well as *Elohim*, but these appear in terms of what is told about them, whereas here the Torah tells us that our forefathers themselves only knew of God as *Shaddai*.

One should consider the fact that this name—which appears often in Genesis and appears here as well, in connection with Genesis—seems to disappear from the time the Torah was given. In the Torah, it only appears in the mouth of the gentile Balaam; it appears very rarely among the prophets and in Psalms, but it is used extensively by Job and his friends—who are not of Israel and do not know of the Torah. Our traditional translations into Aramaic, Onkelos and Yehonatan, left it as it is in their Aramaic texts, evidently because they did not know how—or did not dare—to translate it; and the same is true with the Septuagint, which ignores the word as if it doesn't exist in the text.

The name *Shaddai* has been given different interpretations by the commentators on the Bible and by scholars of the Bible. Most assign it—without a convincing reason—a meaning related to the concepts of might and authority. I will only deal here with one of the interpretations, which is certainly far from the proper meaning, but which expresses a very profound faith and theological reflection—and that is of the greatest of believers in the world of Judaism: Maimonides. He explains *El Shaddai* in terms of "the God for whom it is sufficient" (שדי לו): the God who is sufficient in Himself, whose essence is Himself, and not in functions which He fulfills in relation to the world. That was the perception of our forefathers, of Abraham, Isaac and Jacob, of *El Shaddai*. On this the Midrash comments that our fathers—unlike the generation of Moses—did not demand signs and wonders upon which to base their faith in God. Now though, that Moses was sent to bring the tidings of the redemption to the Israelites, who did not know of God as *El Shaddai*, there was a need to use names of God that represented His actions in the world.

This goes back to the differentiation between the recognition of God in terms of His Godhead, which is the greatest and most profound faith, and the recognition of God in terms of what is known of the function which He has played in history.

After Moses was assigned his mission—after he had already appeared before Pharaoh once, and was ordered to appear together with his brother Aaron a second time before Pharaoh, and to begin the actions that would lead to the redemption of Israel and their being taken out of Egypt—the Torah interrupts the narrative and gives us a short genealogy of Moses and his ancestry, noting specifically various matters that were only hinted at previously. In the *sidra* of *Shemot*, we were only told that Moses was the son of "a man of the house of Levi," who took "a daughter of Levi." Here, in our *sidra*, we learn for the first time that he is Moses, son of Amram, son of Kehat, son of Levi, and that Amram took Yocheved, his aunt, as a wife. We are immediately taken aback, because in the Torah given later by God through Moses, we are told that for a man to take his aunt is one of the most severe prohibitions, for which the penalty is *karet*.

This, though, was before the giving of the Torah, and in terms of the laws pertaining to the Noachides—for whom marrying one's aunt is not prohibited—it was not an illicit union. Nevertheless, the reader cannot escape the association that Moses was born of a union which would later be considered to be prohibited. And here we return to a phenomenon with which we are familiar in the history of our forefathers: Jacob married two sisters (a very long time before the giving of the Torah, but by Torah law this is forbidden), and Abraham and Sarah were half-siblings, with a common father (but different mothers).

The Torah presents to us, and almost stresses the point, that the biological descent—both of our forefathers and of Moses—was not such as are determined by the laws of the Torah which were given later. This comes to teach us that the level which a person achieves in the recognition of God is not dependent on biological factors.

More than that, one of the classic commentators on the Torah, *Chizkuni*, explains why Providence arranged that Moses would be born of a union which would later be considered to be a blemish, even though it was not a blemish at the time—"so that he would not lord it over the people." The danger which lies in wait for every leader and authority figure is that he will begin lording it over those under him, and this is true even if he is a man of God, the faithful shepherd of Israel. It is therefore desirable for a leader to always be forced to remember that there is what might be considered to be a blemish in his genealogy.

And this is the idea that our Sages expressed in their famous statement: "One does not appoint the head of a community unless there is a box of vermin (today one might say "a can of worms") on his back, for (this way), if he becomes haughty, they say to him, 'look behind you.'" In other words, remember who you are. And that is a warning to the leadership in all generations and all eras. In this regard, one may note that behind the anointed kings of Israel lay a string of forbidden sexual unions and forbidden marriages: Ruth the Moabite (who was a descendant of Lot and his daughter), Judah and Tamar his daughter-in-law, David and Bathsheba, Solomon and Na'ama the Ammonite.

BO

The *sidra* of *Bo* is the *sidra* of the exodus from Egypt. And this
sidra discusses two *Pesach*'s, in regard to the great event which, in
fact, was the beginning of the history of the Jewish people: the
Pesach of Egypt, the one-time event which occurred that night
between the 14th and the 15th of the month of *Nissan*, the first month
at the time; and the *Pesach* forever, which was meant to recall to us
the exodus from Egypt, and which for years involved the bringing of
the Paschal sacrifice. Nowadays, we have but a remembrance of that
remembrance: the *Pesach Seder* which is conducted to this day by
the majority of the Jewish people, including those Jews who do not
observe it as a Torah *mitzva*, and not in the form which the *halakha*
sets down.

But it is just the difference between the *Pesach* forever, where a
sacrifice was to be brought, and our *Pesach*, which is the clear
evidence of basic problems of Jewish existence in our times. Here I
will permit myself to present this by relating an event, or, to be more
exact, a discussion, in which I took part a few years ago.

This was a seminar organized by the IDF, a seminar for senior
military officers, which was held in the intermediate days of *Pesach*
in one of the major bases of the IDF, and I was invited to participate
in it. The topic of the seminar was contained in its title: "Judaism,
Jewish People and Jewish State," and this already tells one what the
discussions were all about. The deliberations were very earnest;
various viewpoints and opinions and approaches were presented, but
all the participants treated the topic seriously, as something close to

their hearts, even though they did so from various angles and with different approaches.

I made note of the major and serious fact that a gap has been created between those Jews who observe the *mitzvot* and those who do not, a gap which is not only ideological, but is—even against their will—existential. Two Jews cannot dine at the same table if one—and only one—of them observes the laws of *kashrut*; and families which observe the *mitzvot* cannot intermarry with families which do not, because one of the two prospective spouses (either the male or the female) insists on the observance of the laws of *nidda* and *tevila*, whereas the other prospective spouse rejects the religious discipline of marital life. Nor can Jews who are all aware of their being Jewish, and who know that their fellows are Jewish, work together in the same workplace—because of *Shabbat*. But the kitchen and the table, sex and marital life, and work, constitute the realities of human life; thus we see that we cannot live our lives in common.

One of those taking part in the deliberations, a senior IDF officer, pointed to *Pesach* as a national heritage which we have in common. Even if we have different attitudes toward *Pesach*, we all observe the *Seder*, in one form or another, because we all are conscious of the history of the Jewish people, which started—either historically or symbolically—with the *Pesach* event, and which we all wish to continue. These words were said in total sincerity and with great emotion. To this, I answered him: Imagine that I was not invited here today, to this seminar in one of the IDF bases, but would instead have used the *Pesach* holiday to tour the country, and my wife and I would have been hiking right now. And let us say that today is a very hot *chamsin* day, and thirst and the heat bothered us, and we would have, by chance, come upon the settlement where you live, and we would have entered your farm. Do you know that today we could not even drink a cup of water in your home, because of the *chametz* in your dishes? You are the commander of my sons and grandsons in the army, and today I could not drink a cup of water in your home. *Pesach* today is not a common heritage for us, and, if anything, the festival expresses a deep rift between us.

The man responded to this with deep emotion: It is true that you have mentioned a fact which is frightening, and nevertheless—we have a common awareness of *Pesach*. After all, we all regard *Pesach* as the symbol of the beginning and the continuation of the history of the Jewish people, and we are all united in our desire and in our aim of being a continuing link in this historical chain.

I was forced to point out his error to him, even in regard to this awareness. I told him: I understand and can feel the sincerity in your words and the profound emotion contained within them. For you, *Pesach* is indeed a great symbol of the history of the Jewish people. But for my wife and myself, *Pesach* is not a symbol, but a reality. *Pesach* is not expressed in the fact that we, using certain symbols, in this form or that, remind ourselves of the beginning of the history of the Jewish people. The significance of *Pesach* for us lies in the fact that for seven days we actually live a different life than all the other weeks of the year; for before *Pesach* we, or to be more accurate, my wife, transforms the house in order to prepare it for this festival.

For you, *Pesach* is a sentimental matter, and I am not trying to belittle it: sentiments are of great importance. Nevertheless, for you it is only a sentimental matter, whereas for us, *Pesach* is an existential issue—an issue dealing with our existence in the present, on this day and at this hour—and not a remembrance of an event which may be historical, or again, may be legendary, of 3,500 years ago.

Pesach thus presents us with the most profound problem which confronts the Jewish people and Judaism today.

BESHALACH

Whenever one mentions the *sidra* of *Beshalach*, it brings to mind the great miracle of the splitting of the Sea of Reeds and the loftiness of *Shirat Hayam*—the song sung by the Israelites after crossing the sea. The truth, though, is that this great episode only occupies half of the *sidra*.

The *sidra* is composed of two parts, which appear to belong to two worlds which differ from one another, two worlds in which man's relationship to his existence is very different. And it is interesting—and there is no doubt that it is merely coincidental—that the two parts into which the *sidra* is divided are exactly equal in terms of their number of verses.

Of the 116 verses of the *sidra*, the first 58 verses begin with the exodus from Egypt, "When Pharaoh had let the people go" (*Shemot* 13:17), and end with Miriam too singing the praise of God, "And Miriam answered them, 'Sing you to God, for He has triumphed gloriously; the horse and his rider has he thrown into the sea' (*Shemot* 15:21)." This is the world of miracles, the world of the Godhead, as it were, "invading" natural reality. But the following 58 verses, which begin with, "So Moses led Israel from the Sea of Reeds" (*Shemot* 15:22), is a story which begins three days after the miracle and after the *Shirat Hayam*. In this story, we find ourselves in a totally different world: the splitting of the Sea of Reeds, the revelation by God, the song and the faith (in the first section it states, "they believed in God")—it is as if none of these had happened, and there is not even a hint about them.

In these 58 verses, rather than "they believed" (*Shemot* 14:31), we have "they complained" twice (15:24; 16:2), and in place of the lofty exaltation, we have the gray prose of life: no water to drink, water which is bitter, and no bread to eat. Here too, to be sure, a miracle does occur in that *manna* falls, but it appears in a world which is not a world of exaltation, but rather a world of strife and turmoil. Not only that, but there has been a loss of faith, and the people have the temerity to ask, "Is God among us, or not?"(*Shemot* 17:7).

One receives the impression that the Israelites were not at all impressed by the revelation, in which (according to a late Midrash), "the maidservant at the sea saw [things] that Ezekiel ben Buzi never saw about the Chariot" (i.e., the vision of Ezekiel regarding God's "Chariot"). The people were not impressed; not only that, but the nation was evidently not influenced by the event. It is true that *Shirat Hayam* states, "The nations heard, and were afraid: trembling seized the Philistines. The chieftains of Edom were terrified; the mighty men of Moab, shivering took hold of them" (*Shemot* 15:14–15), but in the second half of that *sidra*, a nation of brigands and plunderers, Amalek, engaged Israel in battle, and evidently had no idea about Israel's closeness to God, who protected it.

From *Beshalach*, we learn something very great, and that is that the miracle and revelation, and even the exaltation of man to sing as a result of the miracle of revelation—all of these are but transitory episodes which have no influence on what occurs later. What endures is not the exaltation of life, but rather the prose of life. And it is just within the framework of that prose of life—"they complained," "they complained"—where there is no water to drink, where the bread is moldy, and where one questions whether "God is with us, or not"—it is just in this framework that the Torah was given to Israel, "there He made for them a statute and an ordinance" (*Shemot* 15:25), and there *Shabbat* was ordained. Before the giving of the Torah and the revelation at Mount Sinai, *Shabbat* was ordained, this being the central institution of Jewish existence in accordance with the Torah.

It is of tremendous importance for comprehending the essence of faith to grasp the fact that miracles and supernatural factors are of no significance religiously, and are, at the least, ineffective as a foundation for faith. The generation which saw the miracles and wonders did not believe. And if we then counter with the verse, "They believed in God, and His servant Moses" (*Shemot* 14:31), that was a transitory faith at the time that they experienced that deliverance; and immediately afterwards, everything was wiped out.

The later sources ponder this fact. The Midrash dares to state that immediately after the people crossed the sea, when they reached the further shore and saw "the Egyptians dead upon the sea shore" (*Shemot* 14:30), they exclaimed: the Egyptians have died. Let us make ourselves an idol and return to Egypt—for idolatry is far more convenient than serving the Lord God of Israel.

Even more than this: a midrashic source states that even at the very time that they were crossing the sea, the people had the idol of Mikha (see *Shoftim* 17, 18) with them. Historically, the idol of Mikha came much later, but conceptually, this Midrash wishes to say that miraculous intervention in man's reality does not help to uproot from him the Evil Desire of idolatry, which is in accordance with his nature.

As opposed to this, we know from history that many generations after this failure, there were many generations in which the masses, not only unique individuals, clung to God and His Torah to the extent of laying down their lives for it. And these were generations which never experienced a Divine revelation, never saw miracles or wonders, had no prophets who spoke the word of God, and not only that, which God did not help and save them in their distress—and yet they believed.

Thus we see that there is no connection between the natural reality in which a person lives and his decision to accept upon himself the Yoke of the Kingdom of Heaven and the Yoke of the Torah and *mitzvot*. This decision can only come from the person himself, and if it does not come from him, if he proves that he is a member of a stiff-necked nation, even Divine intervention cannot bring him to accept the Yoke of the Kingdom of Heaven and the Yoke of the Torah and *mitzvot*.

That is the great message in the world of faith throughout the generations, and therefore it is not coincidental that in a later document on Jewish faith, in *Shulchan Arukh*, the first Hebrew word is "יתגבר— one should make a supreme effort." One needs tremendous effort against one's nature and against one's reality, in order to get up in the morning (and that is the continuation of the words in *Shulchan Arukh*) for the service of God—therefore "one should make a supreme effort."

Faith is not given from outside, and *cannot* be given from outside. It can only grow from man's efforts and from his own decisions.

YITRO

It is very difficult to say anything substantial, in the few minutes available to us, on the great occurrence of the events at Mount Sinai and the giving of the Torah. But one can say something about what is adjacent to this great event.

The *sidra* of *Yitro* does not begin with the giving of the Torah and the events at Mount Sinai, but with Jethro, Moses' father-in-law, coming to Moses and the Israelite camp, and the advice which he gives Moses, whereby Moses prepares a governing and administrative system within the nation by appointing officers of hundreds, of thousands, etc., as judges.

This matter can be examined from various angles. From the text, it appears that at first Moses had no intention of appointing an administrative system among the people, but planned that the administration would be through Divine inspiration that would reach the people through him—through the man who knew God face to face. He also attempted to implement this. We read that he sat "from the morning to the evening" (*Shemot* 18:13), and judged the people by means of the Divine inspiration which he had.

But afterwards he learned from his non-Jewish father-in-law, who had drawn close to Israel, that even leadership based on God's word needs human vessels and tools that derive from the faculties and abilities latent within man himself. Therefore people were chosen to administer and judge the nation, even though the requirements for these—"able men, such as fear God, men of truth, incorruptible" (*Shemot* 18:21)—represent rare human qualities, but human qualities nevertheless. What was not demanded of them was to be divinely inspired.

If that is the case, the administrative and judicial functions based on the Torah are given over to man who acts in accordance with his knowledge and understanding of the Torah of Israel and out of his desire to implement this Torah.

And another important matter in this context: the judges were appointed before the Torah had been given. On what basis were they to judge? After all, a judge must rule in accordance with a law which is already in existence and which the judge recognizes. This implies that even before the written laws were given to Israel, there was already a recognized judicial system, even though it had not yet been written down.

And if we employ the basic terms of Jewish religious thought of a later time—the oral Torah preceded the written Torah. It necessarily had to precede it, for otherwise there could not be a system of administration, government and judiciary as long as the Torah—in which such a system is detailed in writing—was not yet in the hands of the Israelites.

This teaches us a great deal relevant for all time, both in terms of understanding the history of Judaism and in terms of understanding the problems of Judaism throughout all generations, including ours. Without the oral Torah, whose source is the understanding by man of God's Torah and his decisions in accordance with this understanding, an administrative and judicial system in accordance with Torah law is impossible. A condition for arranging the world in accordance with the Torah and the *mitzvot* is that people understand the Torah and that they engage in its study out of a sincere desire to implement it, but this study must be based on their reasoning and must relate to "the needs of the hour."

The oral Torah not only preceded the written Torah in terms of time, as we see from this *sidra*, but also precedes it conceptually. We cannot comprehend the written Torah except through our own understanding of it. And if the oral Torah is consolidated, and in itself becomes a written Torah, then it too must have its own oral Torah. And if such an oral Torah does not exist, the written Torah cannot survive. The great problem of contemporary Judaism is whether an oral Torah in this sense exists nowadays.

MISHPATIM

"These are the laws which you will set before them" (*Shemot* 21:1). This *sidra* contains the major portion of civil and criminal law of the Torah, and, it might appear, is the basis for the entire mighty structure of halakhic practice, as formulated in the order of *Nezikin*—the entire majestic edifice of Torah law as formulated in the Mishna, the Gemara and all of the halakhic ruling from them to the present—to the extent that Torah law is still in effect relating to questions of civil law among Jews who observe the *mitzvot*.

Yet this *halakha*—in regard to civil and criminal law—which is valid in the cognizance and in the reality of Jews who are Torah observant to this day—is very different from the way it appears to be in the language of our *sidra*, if we take the words as they appear literally.

Here we arrive at one of the basic problems, possibly the most basic problem, in understanding the world of the Torah and *mitzvot*, and that is the relationship between the written Torah and the oral Torah; or, if we wish to be more specific, the relationship between the oral Torah and the written Torah.

It is commonly accepted among the naive, and sometimes among those who pretend to be naive, that the entire world of the oral Torah is nothing but the authorized interpretation of the written Torah. But in truth, that is not at all the position of halakhic, talmudic and rabbinic Judaism, but is a Karaite position. The Karaites, too, have their own *halakha*, which they represent as an interpretation of the text of the Torah.

What is unique about halakhic ("rabbinic") Judaism is that it recognizes the autonomy of the oral Torah—which indeed is supported by the written Torah and in formal terms relies on it—but in truth it is the oral Torah which is the one which determines and decides and rules, based on its own criteria. And the authority of the oral Torah to rule based on its own criteria is a basic principle of faith in the historic Judaism of the Torah and *mitzvot*, for it is not the literal meaning of the verse which guides the Jew in observing the Torah and the *mitzvot*, but the world of the oral Torah.

And that was the way these matters were understood by the great of the faith and the great of the *halakha*, when they dealt—and many of them did not deal with this—with understanding the relationship between the oral Torah and the written Torah: we will discuss a few texts of great importance.

Maimonides, the greatest believer and the greatest of *poskim* among the Jewish people, when he deals with the laws of torts, on the one hand understands the verse of "an eye for an eye" and that of "as he causes a blemish in a person, so will it be done to him," as meaning exactly what the words say in the Torah; and he explains the rationality and the ethical basis behind these laws. At the same time, though, the great *posek* knows that even the earliest sources of the oral Torah—from the Mishna on—state that the person who inflicts a wound upon his fellow must pay for the pain, damage, medical expenses, loss of income, and humiliation, but this is a financial penalty, not a bodily punishment.

And Maimonides states, in continuing his explanation of why the Torah states what it does: "Do not bother your mind that we punish here by making the person pay." Who are the "we" Maimonides refers to? "We" are the Jewish people, who rule in accordance with the Torah law. We punish the person here by making him pay. "For the intention now"—and in using the word "now" he refers to himself and his work—"is to give the reason for the written text, not to give reasons for the oral Torah." The oral Torah has its own reasons. It is not just an interpretation of the written Torah; and it is the oral Torah which obligates us.

And now we leap forward 500–600 years, to one of the most prominent figures of rabbinic Judaism—which is based on both the written and the oral Torah—to the Gaon of Vilna. And he does not say that "an eye for an eye" means a financial penalty. Rather, he writes: "the *halakha* uproots the Torah text." This expression already appears in the Talmud regarding certain details, but the Gaon extends this and says: "So it is in most of this section (the *sidra* of *Mishpatim*) and so with a number of chapters in the Torah." And here, the Gaon lays down a major principle of belief: "And it is the greatness of our oral Torah, that it is the *halakha* to Moses from Sinai, and it is turned as clay to the seal."

This last statement, "it is turned as clay to the seal," is a metaphor taken from the book of Job (38:14). The image is clear: the writing on a seal is a mirror image, so that when one uses the seal, the imprint is correct. The analogy is that there are things in the oral Torah which contradict what the written Torah states, but that is "the *halakha* to Moses from Sinai." In other words, from the outset ("from Sinai") the oral Torah was given the authority to rule as it rules, even though it appears as a seal is to the writing that is derived from that seal.

Finally, let us quote *Ketzot Hachoshen*, a very late commentary on *Shulchan Arukh*, which is the basis for rabbinic rulings to this day in that world where rabbinic rulings still exist in civil matters. *Ketzot Hachoshen* notes that the rabbinic authorities in the field of *halakha* have the right to rule in accordance with their understanding of the Torah, for we were given the Torah to use as we understand it. He says—and these words are most significant—that everyday practical *halakha* could not have been given directly by God, whereby we would be tied to it in exactly the way it is written and read: "For had everything been in writing from God, and should we have to understand it, it would have been incomprehensible to us, for how could the human intellect understand God's Torah? But *the oral Torah is ours*," and that is why we understand it, we can study it, we can deal with it, we can develop it, in order to observe God's Torah.

We have the authority to do this, and not only authority, but the obligation to do so. God's Torah is not in the Jewish people's possession if they do not study it in accordance with human understanding on the basis of the intention to implement this Torah.

TERUMAH

"They will take Me an offering…. Let them make Me a sanctuary; and I will dwell among them" (*Shemot* 25:2, 8). With these verses, the Torah begins the narrative of the building of the sanctuary and the construction of its utensils. This section includes the entire *sidrot* of *Terumah* and *Vayakhel*, and parts of the *sidrot* of *Tetzaveh*, *Ki Tisa*, and *Pekudei*. The sanctuary and its appurtenances were meant to serve as the framework for serving God—to the extent that this was represented by the sacrifices, the instructions on which are contained in the book of Leviticus. The Torah devotes between 250 to 300 verses to the construction of the sanctuary and its vessels (and I am ignoring here approximately 90 other verses in *Tetzaveh* and *Pekudei*, which deal with the preparation of the garments for the priests, which were also used for the sacrifices).

As opposed to this, the first *parasha* of the Torah describes the creation of the universe and all in it, heaven and earth and all their hosts, the sun and the moon and the stars, including our planet, with its seas and mountains and everything which grows on it, as well as all the creatures living on it, including man himself—and to all of this, the Torah devotes 31 verses.

And even if we add to this, in accordance with the Torah, that the completion of the creation was *Shabbat*, we still only have a total of 34 verses. And if we include the dedication of the sanctuary as representing its completion, this paralleling the completion of the Creation by *Shabbat*, we will have close to 400 verses which deal with a portable structure which had 20 planks along its length and 8 planks along its width, and which was not even covered by a roof, but by curtains. And the discussions about the sanctuary—the description of the wood and of the construction, occupy ten times as much space in the Torah as does the creation of the entire universe and all in it.

How can we understand this? Indeed, it has a very profound meaning.

The Torah did not come to give man information on the construction of the world, but to tell him something about the significance of the existence of man himself within the framework of the world: and the significance of this is that one must serve God. The world in itself, as we recognize it, was given to us as something that God had created; whatever is—is, regardless of how man relates to it. That is why all of creation is indifferent in regard to goals, duties or obligations, and even in regard to man's beliefs, views, opinions, expectations, hopes and visions.

But this small sanctuary was not a natural given, but the product of human activity in accordance with a *mitzva* of the Torah. "They will take Me an offering": man is required to give it. "They will make Me a sanctuary": people must make it. As far as man is concerned, there is no importance or significance in regard to those things that exist by the nature of creation.

That means that only what is related to the tasks imposed on man, and not what is given to him naturally—i.e., only expresses a demand made upon man, or obligations imposed upon him—it is this that is of importance and significance. The world and all in it lack significance, and if I know it as we know it from scientific research, there is nothing left for me to ask about my relation to it. But in the world of values, the *mitzvot* imposed upon man, the obligations that man accepts upon himself—these are not givens of nature. And this sanctuary, which has no meaning except for the goal of serving God, and man constructs it for that purpose—it is that which symbolizes the service of God as the highest value.

"They will make Me a sanctuary, that I may (or: "and I shall") dwell in their midst." When people construct a sanctuary in honor of

God, they bring the *Shekhina* down to dwell among them. The world acquires significance and value, if within its framework people serve God. It is not the world in itself that is significant: what is significant is the service of God in the world. And that is why the *parasha* of the sanctuary is so much more prominent in the Torah than is the *parasha* of creation.

Another note on the vessels in the sanctuary. Staves were prepared whereby the sanctuary might be carried from one place to another. In regard to the copper altar, the gold altar, the table for the show-bread and the *menora*, the staves were only placed in the rings made for them when there was need to carry these vessels. The exception to this was the ark with the Two Tablets, from which the staves were never removed.

What is the meaning of this? All the vessels used in the Divine service were generally meant to be in a specific place, "the place that God will choose," where the sanctuary would be located. Thus the staves were only meant for unusual circumstances which required the vessels to be moved. But the ark, which symbolized the Torah, was by its very essence made to be moved from one place to another, and that is why the staves were fixed in it permanently. The Torah is not bound to a specific place. It is the Torah of man as man, wherever he is found. And that is why the ark was always ready in a form which showed that by its nature it could be moved.

The midrashic tradition expressed this idea in various forms. And by this it also explains why the Torah was not given in the Land of Israel, but rather outside a permanent human settlement, in the desert—in no man's land. The Midrash uses the Greek word *demosion*, meaning public property. The Torah is not the Torah of a specific land, but is the Torah of man *qua* man wherever he may be. That is why the Torah was deliberately given in the *demosion*, so that it should be known that it was meant for all, just as the desert is ownerless and is open to all.

TETZAVEH

Already in the previous discussion, in the section dealing with the command to construct the sanctuary, I noted one of the first verses in this section: "Let them make Me a sanctuary; and I will dwell among them" (*Shemot* 25:8). The sanctuary was not God's domicile, but expressed the fact that Israel assumed the obligation to serve God. They made a sanctuary in honor of God—and God dwelled among them, not in this house.

And at the end of the great *parasha* of the command to build the sanctuary and to prepare the vessels of the sanctuary and the clothes for the priests, with which the majority of the *sidra* of *Tetzaveh* deals, is a verse which parallels the verse at the beginning: "I will dwell among the Israelites, and I will be their God, and they will know that I am their God who took them out of Egypt to dwell among them, I am their God" (*Bereishit* 29:45–46).

The sanctuary and what followed, the glorious temple which came after the portable tent, was not the dwelling place of God. On the contrary, a few hundred years later, Isaiah (66:1) stated: "Thus says God, 'The heaven is My throne, and the earth is My footstool: where is a house that you can build for Me and where is the place of My rest?'"

So too, when the Temple was dedicated, King Solomon exclaimed, "The heaven and heaven of heavens cannot contain You; how much less this house that I have built?" (I *Melakhim* 8:27). True believers, who attempted to comprehend God and to understand what the Godhead is, admitted that man cannot build a home and sanctuary for God, but he can accept upon himself to serve God, which he symbolizes in what he does with the intention of serving God.

But one should add something else, and that too is discussed at length in the midrashic literature. As far as the sanctuary was concerned, when Moses was commanded to build it, the stress—and this is repeated numerous times—was on "they will make….," "they will make….," "they will make….": they will make the sanctuary, they will make the curtains, they will make the copper altar, they will make the gold altar, etc.

All of this was made by the hand of man, and there was no Divine intervention in the construction of the sanctuary. Everything was man-made, and we even know which men made it: Bezalel b. Uri and Oholiav b. Ahisamakh, who were craftsmen. The *Shekhina* dwelling in Israel came about as a result of the work of men. Inspiration does not come from the outside. Inspiration comes about as a result of what man does in order to receive it. Without man's actions, it is possible that there will not be any inspiration.

In the command to Moses to hand the work over to two experts (and not only to them, but to all of Israel: "They will take Me an offering, of every man that gives it willingly with his heart" [*Shemot* 25:2], all were partners in this project, including also "every woman that had the talent to spin with her hands" [*Shemot* 35:25])—within the framework of this command, we are told something about what would occur after the command was obeyed. After you build the sanctuary, "I will meet with you there, and I will commune with you from above the cover" (*Shemot* 25:22). God's word to man would be given through Moses, and would be given above the cover—the *kaporet*—whose length was 2½ cubits and whose width was 1½ cubits. It is to these dimensions that the *Shekhina*, as it were, reduced Itself when It spoke to Moses. As opposed to this, Solomon said, "The heaven and heaven of heavens cannot contain You; how much less this house that I have built?"

If that is so, what changed? Why, in the sanctuary, was the *Shekhina* reduced to an area of 2½ by 1½ cubits, whereas afterwards the entire world and everything in it was insufficient to contain It?

The answer to this is given in Aramaic, in a parable which seems to have been popular among the people. It is given as a conversation between a man and his wife, or between a lover and his beloved, and they say, or he says to her, or she says to him:

> "When our love was strong, we could both sleep together on the edge of a sword (or, as another version has it, "the edge of a sword would not have been too narrow for us to sleep on it"), for there was great love between us. Now, when the love between us has ceased or weakened, a bed the width of 60 cubits is not enough for us. Each of us is afraid that the other is taking too much of the 60 cubit-wide bed." When the love between Israel and its God was intense, the *Shekhina* could reduce Itself and come into contact with Israel on the *kaporet*, in an area of less than 4 square cubits. Now that this love has become weaker—"the heaven and heaven of heavens cannot contain You; how much less this house that I have built?"

The closeness between God and man is conditional on the degree of love that man has for God. In the spirit of the verse said in the *Shema*, which is the key verse of faith: "You will love the Lord your God with all your heart and with all your soul and with all your might." Then the *Shekhina* can reduce Itself to the area of human existence. If not—the world and all in it are not large enough for the *Shekhina*.

KI TISA

We are unable to give an evaluation of the different *sidrot* in the Torah, to its 54 *sidrot*. Every word in the Torah is worth every other. Nevertheless, from a psychological perspective, we cannot refrain from being deeply impressed by certain *sidrot*. And it would appear to me that there is no *sidra* like *Ki Tisa* in terms of the impression it makes regarding our understanding of faith—which is the basic subject of the entire Torah.

The episode of the golden calf comes forty days after the events at Mount Sinai. At Mount Sinai, we are told that the people exclaimed, "We will do and we will obey" (*Shemot* 24:7). Forty days later, they made the calf, exclaiming, "These are your gods, O Israel" (*Shemot* 32:4).

From this we see that faith, the true recognition of the God of Israel, is not imparted to a person, nor even to a nation—neither to the individual nor to the community—by inspiration which comes from the outside; even the revelation of God's *Shekhina* was not sufficient. The faith of which we are told at Mount Sinai was counterfeit. It was an expression of a temporary impression. The people saw this great sight, but it did not leave any long-lasting impact on them.

Thus we see that faith must come from the person himself; even the revelation of the *Shekhina* is not sufficient to bring a person to true faith. This is expressed in the entire biblical narrative. Even after the revelation of the *Shekhina*—which was not only at Mount Sinai but throughout the story of the exodus from Egypt, the splitting of the Sea of Reeds, the *manna* falling, etc., and after all those forty years of living miraculously in the desert—it was not enough. Moses, on the day that he died, after these forty years, told Israel, "even while I am yet alive with you this day, you have been rebellious against God" (*Devarim* 31:27). Afterwards, for about twenty generations, there were prophets in Israel, through whom God's *Shekhina* spoke to the people, and not a single prophet was successful in making a single person mend his ways.

As opposed to this, we are familiar with Jewish history thousands of years after the Bible: we are aware of tens of generations in which masses of Jews—not individuals—cleaved to God and His Torah to the extent of even giving their lives for their belief. And these were generations in which the *Shekhina* never revealed Itself, and they never saw miracles or wonders, nor did they have prophets through whom the *Shekhina* spoke, and God did not save them and did not aid them in their distress and did not help them—and they did believe.

The events of the revelation at Mount Sinai, and, as opposed to this, the story of the golden calf, prove that faith is not acquired except through the individual's personal decision: the acceptance of the Yoke of Heaven. The acceptance of the Yoke of Heaven cannot be imposed on a person from the outside, and it is of no value if it is imposed from the outside. It is true that there is a midrashic view (which in my opinion is erroneous) that God suspended Mount Sinai over the Jewish people in order to have them accept the Torah. But even if we accept this legend, the Torah testifies that this did not help.

The story of the golden calf and what follows it is linked to another major incident. Moses breaks the Two Tablets after he descends from the mountain and sees what is going on. Now, if the concept of holiness applies (and many in our days use the word freely in regard to human problems, interests, needs or achievements, to the nation,

the land, the state, etc.) in human existence, it certainly applied to
the tablets, which were "the work of God," with "the writing of God
engraved on them," and yet Moses smashed them when he saw who
the nation was and what the nation was.

A lack of time prevents me from expanding on the tremendous
significance of this, and I will content myself with quoting one of
the great Sages of our time, R. Meir Simcha Hakohen of Dvinsk,
who, in my opinion, was one of the few profound religious thinkers
on faith in the rabbinic world in recent generations. Below are his
comments on Moses breaking the tablets:

> Torah and faith are the main aspects of Jewish faith, and all the sancti-
> ties—*Eretz Israel* and Jerusalem and the Temple—are but details of
> the Torah and were sanctified through the holiness of the Torah....
> There is no difference for all Torah matters either in regard to place or
> time. It is the same in *Eretz Israel* and outside the land.... Do not think
> that the sanctuary and the Temple are holy objects in their own right.
> Far be it! God dwells among His people, and if they are like Adam
> who violated the covenant, all their sanctity is removed and they are
> profane objects, where the evildoers came and desecrated them....
> More than that: even the tablets, with the writing of God, are not holy
> in themselves, but are so only because of you, if you observe them.
> Then, when the bride whored under her bridal canopy [this is a strong
> midrashic statement, which refers to the incident of the golden calf so
> soon after the revelation at Mount Sinai]—they [the tablets] were con-
> sidered as base pottery, for they have no sanctity in themselves, but
> only become such when you observe them. In conclusion [the follow-
> ing words should be written in large letters before our eyes]: there is
> noting in the world which is holy...only God is holy...for nothing in
> creation is holy in itself, only in terms of the observance of the Torah
> in accordance with God's will.... All sanctity is due to a command that
> the Creator commanded [us] to worship Him.

VAYAKHEL-PEKUDEI

Vayakhel and *Pekudei*—these two *sidrot* appear to be a repetition of *Terumah* and *Tetzaveh*, and we have already noted the importance and significance of the space and the detail that the Torah devotes to the construction of the sanctuary, as compared to the space it devotes to the creation of the world. We explained that a comparison between the two teaches us that the religious status of the individual to God is not influenced by his knowledge of God's actions toward the world, but by his serving of God in the world.

In repeating all of these ideas, we find in *Vayakhel* and *Pekudei* a very profound hint concerning this concept. Before the Torah repeats the command regarding the construction of the sanctuary and of the implementation of that command, we find three verses, which interrupt the flow of the *parasha* and which raise an issue which, it would seem to appear, has nothing to do with the matter at hand, and that is the topic of *Shabbat*.

Not only is *Shabbat* presented here as a clear interruption in the midst of this long chapter of hundreds of verses dealing with the sanctuary, but it is dealt with in a unique fashion, for which there is almost no counterpart in the entire system of laws and statutes which were given to Israel: "Moses gathered all the community of the Israelites, and said to them, 'This is what God has commanded, that you should do' (*Shemot* 35:1)." Here, in the very midst of the details regarding the sanctuary, Moses gathers together all the people and says to them, "Six days will work be done, but on the seventh day there will be to you an holy day, a *Shabbat* of rest to God:

whosoever does work therein will be put to death. You will not kindle fire throughout your habitations on *Shabbat*."

And immediately afterwards we return, as if there had been no interruption whatsoever, to words that have already become almost rote: "Moses spoke to all the community of the Israelites, 'This is what God commanded, "Take you from among you an offering to God""'(*Shemot* 35:4–5)—an offering for the building of the sanctuary. And from this point on, the Torah returns to the construction of the sanctuary. What is the meaning of these verses on *Shabbat* at this point, with the powerful introduction: "Moses gathered all the community of the Israelites together"?

Shabbat is the supreme symbol that the world, with everything in it, is God's, "For in six days God made heaven and earth, the sea, and all that is in them, and rested the seventh day" (*Shemot* 20:11). Therefore, you who are engaged here in the work related to the sanctuary, do not forget what the significance is of this work. The work related to the sanctuary is carried out entirely by people. There is no Divine intervention, nor are there any miraculous acts. The materials used in the sanctuary are brought by human beings, the work is carried out by human beings, the chief artisans are mentioned by name, and the words, "you will make" and "he made" are repeated innumerable times. Do not forget before whom all of these things are being made—they are being made before the One who spoke and created the world. It is in this context that *Shabbat* and the rigor of the laws regarding *Shabbat* are mentioned, because *Shabbat* is a reminder of the act of creation, a sign of the creation of the world by God.

One can still ask: Why did the Torah stress the prohibition against lighting a fire at this point, of all the categories of work forbidden on *Shabbat*? On this question, I can only offer a hypothesis. The use of fire was the beginning of human civilization, and every type of work or labor meant to produce from nature anything which nature does not supply to man directly, or, in other words, all the products of civilization—traces back ultimately to the fact that prehistoric man, tens of thousands of years ago, learned how to make fire. At the beginning of *Vayakhel,* all of human civilization is portrayed as illuminated by the appreciation of the *Shabbat* day, which is the symbol of the fact that the world is God's world.

It is also possible to find a hint on another topic in the two *sidrot* which repeat the work on the sanctuary—a hint that here the service of God by man in the world is contrasted with the creation of the world by God. Thus we see that the end of the creation is marked by one of the most commonly quoted verses, "The heaven and the earth were completed, and all within them" (*Bereishit* 2:1). And the completion of the sanctuary uses the exact same formula: "Thus was all the work of the tabernacle of the Tent of Assembly finished" (*Bereishit* 39:32). It is difficult to assume that this is not deliberate: "The heavens and the earth were finished" parallels "Thus was all the work of the tabernacle of the Tent of Assembly completed." But not only that—once "the heaven and the earth and all within them were completed," we are told: "God blessed the seventh day, and sanctified it" (*Bereishit* 2:3); and after the sanctuary was completed we are told, "and Moses blessed them" (*Bereishit* 39:43). And here, "them" refers to those involved in the work on the sanctuary. "Heaven and earth...were completed" parallels "the work on the sanctuary...[was] completed;" and "God blessed the seventh day" parallels "Moses blessed them." The intended conformity between the two is obvious.

We will conclude with a midrashic confrontation between the work on the sanctuary in our *sidra* and the work on the golden calf in the previous *sidra*. The Israelites were commanded, "They will bring Me an offering" (*Shemot* 25:2), an offering of everything needed for the work on the sanctuary. And afterwards, in the implementation of the command, we are told that "every one of a generous heart" brought his offering.

The Midrash, which pays scrupulous attention to the wording of the biblical narration, remarks that when summoned "for the good," i.e., for the worship of God, for the work on the sanctuary, "every one of a generous heart" brought an offering; this is not a collective noun pertaining to the entire nation or community. On the other hand, when the people themselves decided to worship what they considered to be a god, namely the golden calf, the Torah states that, "All the people broke off the golden earrings" (*Shemot* 32:3) for this purpose.

Thus when it was "for the good," only those of a generous heart reacted, whereas "for the evil" engendered a response by the entire nation.

The reason for this is that worshipping God does not come from a natural impulse within man; it requires of him a spiritual effort in order to overcome his nature and to accept upon himself the Yoke of the Kingdom of Heaven. With idolatry, in contrast, man has a natural urge to engage in it. In a very late document in the world of Judaism, about three thousand years after the giving of the Torah, in the *Shulchan Arukh*, which expounds on the Yoke of the Torah and *mitzvot* in all its details—the first word in the Hebrew text is the Hebrew word for "making oneself strong" for the service of God.

One does not need to make an effort to serve the golden calf, whereas serving God requires strength. But already in Psalms we find those who serve God being referred to as, "those that excel in strength, that do His *mitzvot*" (*Tehillim* 103:20). Man is by nature driven to serve the golden calf, whereas observing God's word demands great strength.

CHUMASH

VAYIKRA

VAYIKRA

Vayikra and *Tzav*—these are the two *sidrot* on the laws of the sacrifices, which gave an expression to the worship of God in biblical times. We will not deal here with the major issue of explaining the entire topic of the sacrifices and the reasons for them, which occupy a major place in both the world of *halakha* and that of thought on matters of belief in Jewish theology. In the minutes available to us, we will deal with the verse which begins the exposition of the subject. "He called to Moses, and God spoke to him out of the Tent of Assembly, 'Speak to the Israelites, and say to them.'"

This opening is unique. There is no analogy to it in the entire Torah. We are accustomed to the opening, "God spoke to Moses...." Here, though, we have, "He called Moses, and God spoke to him out of the Tent of Assembly...."

Many sources, in the Talmud, the Midrash, and in later thought, discuss the fact that it is possible to deduce from this verse (although this is not the literal meaning, but is homiletical) that the voice, the voice of God, was heard in the Tent of Assembly, but was not heard outside it. "The voice would come to the ears of Moses in the Tent of Assembly, and the voice would stop and would not go outside the tent." This is one of the versions in the different sources, some of which *Rashi* also quotes.

"He called to Moses"—the voice spread out and came to his ears, and all of Israel did not hear. One might imagine they did not hear the voice calling out. It therefore states: "the voice to him"—Moses heard, but all of Israel did not hear, for the voice would stop and would not go outside the tent. One might imagine this was because the voice was low (and that was why it was impossible to hear the voice outside the Tent of Assembly). It therefore states: "the voice"—what is "the voice"? It is the voice which is explained by, "The voice of God is powerful; the voice of God is full of majesty. The voice of God breaks the cedars" (*Tehillim* 29:4). If that is so, why does it state "from the Tent of Assembly"? From this we deduce that it was a voice which stopped. Even though this was a voice which shattered the cedars, it would stop outside the Tent of Assembly.

In other words: God's voice was only heard by whoever was in the Tent of Assembly, the place where man communed with God. Of course God's voice thunders over the earth, but a person doesn't hear it unless he is in the Tent of Assembly and is communing with God.

In another source we find: "The very loud voice was limited to the courtyard, and was not heard outside it, for only one who is involved in the worship of God can hear the voice of God." This refers to one who accepts the Yoke of the Torah and *mitzvot*. A person does not assume the Yoke of the Torah and *mitzvot* because God's voice reaches him, but God's voice reaches a person who accepts upon himself the Yoke of the Torah and *mitzvot*.

And this is a very important point. Faith is not given to man from the outside, nor even by the revelation of God and hearing God speak to oneself. A person does not achieve faith unless he makes the decision to enter the Tent of Assembly. And if not—he does not hear the voice of God, even if this voice thunders throughout the entire world.

And now for one detail in the laws of the sacrifices in the *sidra* of *Vayikra*. In the *sidra*, we have the details of the laws of the *chatat*— the sacrifice brought for committing a sin through negligence (i.e., by acting out of ignorance of the law or by mistaking something which is forbidden for something which is permitted). There we are told, "If a soul will sin through negligence," "if the anointed (i.e., high) priest sins according to the guilt of the people," "and if the whole community of Israel sin through negligence," "when a ruler (*nasi*) has sinned" (*Vayikra* 4:2, 3, 13, 22).

The high priest, who is the representative of the entire community in performing the service in the sanctuary, is of course no more than human, and he too can err and commit a sin through negligence, and he too must bring a *chatat*. But here the Torah formulation is strange: "if the anointed priest sins according to the guilt of the people." What is the meaning of "according to" in this verse?

In all the sources, from the talmudic and on, in all the commentaries on the Torah, there are two different approaches to understanding this, and they can be expressed in a statement of the Sages which, although it does not deal necessarily with this verse, expresses the idea: Does the community—in other words, the social, cultural and moral level of a certain population at a given time—correspond to the ruler (in other words, is it the leadership which molds the nation) or does the ruler correspond to the community (is the leadership molded by the people)? Or, to put it in terms used by various nations, does this mean that every nation gets the rulers it deserves?

There are thus two possible approaches to "if the anointed priest sins according to the guilt of the people": Does this mean that the sin of the high priest, which he sins through negligence (i.e., an error made by the leadership), is what causes the people to sin? Does the sin of the anointed priest bring the people to sin as well? Or is the meaning that the sin of the people causes the anointed priest to sin? In other words, does he sin because the people sinned?

And we return to a problem which has tremendous social and political significance: Should one blame the corruption of a nation on its rulers? Or is it that the nature of the leadership is such because the people are such? And there is a vast difference between the two: in the first case, we say that the situation can be remedied by a change of leadership, but one cannot change a nation, and therefore, in the second case, the remedy can only come about by people improving themselves.

There is another point I would like to touch on—among the many that can be mentioned on this *sidra*: what the Torah states in regard to the *nasi*. A *nasi* is a political ruler, including a king. The prophets, in fact, refer to the king, on occasion, as a *nasi*. I have already mentioned that in all the other cases the Torah states "if" the individual or the community or the anointed priest sins. With the *nasi*, though, it states, "*when* the *nasi* sins."

Regarding this, we find a most profound statement in our sources. Every Jew, even the high priest and even the entire community, can possibly sin, but this does not necessarily have to be the case. That is why the Torah states *"if"* in each case. In the case of the *nasi*, on the other hand, he will definitely sin. Why? Because he is a *nasi*, and the very fact that one has power leads the person to be corrupted. Thus, in this case the Torah does not describe sin as a possibility, but from the outset states: "*when* a *nasi* sins." There is no doubt that a *nasi* will sin. It is impossible to have a government, it is impossible to have ruling power, where the ruler will not be involved in a sin, and that is the general way the Torah relates to every regime: it recognizes it and its authority, but—in the words of a well-known talmudic saying—"respect it and suspect it."

TZAV

This time I would like not to discuss the *sidra* itself, which is the *sidra* of *Tzav*, but the *haftara* of this *sidra*, which has a profound link with the *sidra*, and from it we will be able to learn its meaning. This year, *Tzav* is read on *Shabbat Hagadol*, the *Shabbat* preceding *Pesach*, and therefore the *haftara* is not the specific one for *Tzav* but rather the one for *Shabbat Hagadol*, but we will discuss the *haftara* of the *sidra* in regular years, when it does not occur on *Shabbat Hagadol*.

Tzav, following what preceded it in *Vayikra*, deals with the rules of the sacrifices. The sacrificial ritual plays a major role in worshipping God—or at least it did in biblical times. The topic of the sacrifices, both as text and as practice, always allowed for great errors in understanding, which related the worship of God to the act of bringing the sacrifice, rather than to the intention which must accompany the act.

Therefore, when the *haftarot* were ordained for the various *sidrot*, the *haftara* of *Tzav* was chosen from Jeremiah, where the prophet explains the true significance of the sacrifice. And this is what Jeremiah says: "Thus says God of hosts, the God of Israel; Add your burnt offerings (*olot*) to your sacrifices (*zevahim*), and eat flesh" (*Yirmiyahu* 7:21). (*Zevahim* refers to the *shelamim* sacrifices; the *olot* were burned up entirely on the altar, whereas in the case of the *shelamim*, part was burned on the altar, and the rest was eaten. Eating the meat of the *shelamim* is part of the ritual of bringing the sacrifice.)

The prophet, in the name of God, speaks disparagingly of the sacrifice:

> Add your burnt offerings to your sacrifices, and eat flesh. For the day that I brought them out of Egypt I spoke not to your fathers, nor commanded them anything in matters of burnt offerings or sacrifices: But this is what I commanded them, "Obey Me, and I will be your God, and you will be My people: and walk in all the ways that I have commanded you".... But they did not obey nor lend me their ear.
> (*Yirmiyahu* 7:21–24)

In this connection, Jeremiah accuses the people of various crimes, including stealing, murdering, whoring and perjuring.

At first, this seems to be puzzling, for when speaking of the exodus from Egypt, we generally refer to the entire forty years in the desert; in any case, that is the customary term applied to the forty years in which the Torah was given to Israel. In the Torah, the various burnt offerings and sacrifices occupy a very prominent part, and in my talks in the last few weeks I explained the tremendous part that the sanctuary plays in the Torah. Yet this was known to Jeremiah no less than it is to us. Therefore, what does he mean when he says in the name of God, "For the day that I brought them out of Egypt I spoke not to your fathers, nor commanded them anything in matters of burnt offerings or sacrifices"?

Here we must understand "the day that I brought them out of the land of Egypt" to mean literally that—the actual day that God took Israel out of Egypt. At that time, indeed, the Israelites had not yet been commanded concerning the sacrifices. Nor can one point out the paschal lamb preceding the exodus, for that was not a sacrifice at all. None of the lamb was sacrificed to God. Rather, it was a family meal, which symbolized the exodus to freedom. The rules regarding the sacrifices were only given later, when Israel were in the desert.

Therefore, indeed, on the day that God took Israel out of Egypt, He did not speak to them of burnt offerings or other sacrifices. But, the prophet adds, God did command them something: "Obey Me, and I will be your God, and you will be My people: and walk in all the ways that I have commanded you." If, however, this verse refers to the actual day that Israel left Egypt, one cannot say that on that very day God commanded them to "walk in the ways I have commanded you."

What were they commanded at that moment? What does Jeremiah refer to when he says, in the name of God, that at that time He commanded them about the most important point of all? We do not find any reference to this in the story of the exodus itself.

We find the explanation for this in Jeremiah itself, in a different place, in chapter 34, which deals with one of the most significant issues in the history of Israel and the history of faith in Israel: the law governing the freeing of slaves in the seventh year. The terrible sin of the people at the time of Zedekiah was that, while they did free their slaves, they immediately afterwards seized them for another term of slavery. It is because of this that Jeremiah predicts destruction upon Jerusalem, the king and the people; one of the harshest prophecies from the prophet of the destruction.

Jeremiah begins his prophecy with the words, "Thus says God, the God of Israel" (*Yirmiyahu* 34:13). I do not think that it is a mere coincidence that Jeremiah uses the identical words he had used a number of years earlier, in regard to the burnt offerings and sacrifices. There the prophet had stated, "Thus says God of hosts, the God of Israel; 'Add your burnt offerings to your sacrifices, and eat flesh' (*Yirmiyahu* 7:21)." Here again, he exclaims, "Thus says God, the God of Israel, 'I made a covenant with your fathers the day that I brought them out of Egypt [the same words appear in both quotations], out of the land of slavery, saying: At the end of seven years let go every man his brother a Hebrew, who has been sold to you' (34:13–14)."

Jeremiah tells us something that is not told in the Torah: that the day that God freed Israel from Egypt, He commanded them to free the slaves in the seventh year. What God had said to the people on the day that He took them out of Egypt, "I will be your God, and you will be My people, and walk in all the ways that I have commanded you" (*Yirmiyahu* 7:23), was a reference to the freeing of slaves. And it is the nullification of this that led to the prophecy of the total destruction.

From this we see that the sacrifices are not the essence of the worship of God, but come to symbolize the worship of God by the people who observe this covenant. This covenant was not the burnt sacrifices and the other sacrifices, but the freeing of the slaves.

Now for a note on a single verse in this *sidra*. The last paragraph in the *sidra* of *Tzav* refers to preparing Aaron and his sons to consecrate them for the priesthood, and it begins with the words, "Take Aaron and his sons with him, and the garments, and the anointing oil...."(*Vayikra* 8:2). Here too, the classical sources ask what is meant by this. What is conveyed in the words, "and his sons with him"? We know that the priesthood is something which is passed down by heredity: if Aaron was consecrated for the priesthood, his sons too would inherit the priesthood from him. To this day, there are Jews who stem from that lineage, and they are the *kohanim*.

Here too, the Midrash says something of great interest. The priesthood given to Aaron was indeed inherited by his sons, and we find nothing else like it in the Torah. The Torah given to any Jew is not handed down by inheritance. Each generation must study it on its own, and does not inherit it from its fathers. Therefore, the Torah states, "Take Aaron and his sons with him" (*Vayikra* 8:2), for we have nothing of Moses' sons continuing in his mission; they are Jews as all other Jews. Thus we also see that the sons of Eli, the high priest, did not inherit the high priesthood, and we are told clearly that they deviated from the straight path and were rejected. Similarly, in the case of the prophet Samuel, who at a later time was compared by the prophets to Moses (Jeremiah speaks of Moses and

Samuel as the great leaders of the Jewish people)—even about Samuel it states that his sons did not inherit from him either prophecy or leadership, and they did not even walk in his ways.

In other words, one does not inherit those great values of faith and of worship of God: Samuel was not granted having his sons inherit this. But there is one case which is the exception—the priesthood given to Aaron, which is passed on from one generation to the next. Therefore the Torah found it necessary to explain this: "Take Aaron and his sons with him.... And gather all the community together to the door of the Tent of Assembly." This too has something to teach us for all times.

SHEMINI

On the eighth day of the festival celebrating the consecration of the sanctuary and the institution of the priesthood in Israel for all time, meant as the establishment of the procedure for the worship of God throughout the ages, Aaron and his sons are consecrated into the priesthood. Both Aaron and his sons are anointed to the priesthood to show that it will be an institution which will be transmitted from father to son—and this was something which Moses was not granted, for his sons did not continue with his Torah. There is no continuity in the Torah from one generation to another, unless the people themselves continue it.

The priesthood, though, as mentioned, was given to Aaron and his sons, and these, his two oldest sons, died on that day, died in the sanctuary, as we read in a later *sidra*, "When they approached God [illicitly], and died" (*Vayikra* 16:1). In *Shemini*, we are given the reason for this: "They presented illicit fire before God, which He did not command them" (*Vayikra* 10:1). To whom did they sacrifice? To the Lord, God of Israel, whom they wished to worship, when they "drew near before God." In no way was this comparable to the worship of the golden calf, and nevertheless, just as many people died following the worship of the golden calf, here two of Aaron's sons died.

What is the meaning of the "illicit fire" which they offered before God? If we read the words as written, without any punctuation, the implication is that they did something which they were not commanded to do. Should a person deserve the death penalty simply for doing something that he was not commanded to do?

But the *masora*—the Geonic era addition of vowels and cantillation to the biblical texts—offers us a certain hint: the word "not" (*lo* in the Hebrew), in the phrase "did not command," has an extremely rare cantillation sign, the *merkhah kefulah*, and that was why some of the commentators understand the sentence to mean "illicit fire which He commanded them not to bring." In other words, their act was not one which they were not commanded about at all, but was one which violated a specific order for them *not* to do as they subsequently did.

But this is more *derash* than *peshat*, and the literal meaning here may just be more profound. Just as it is possible for a person to be drawn to regard the calf as god even where his intention was to worship God ("these are your gods, O Israel"—and the calf became god), the worship of God itself, if not performed with one's awareness that he is obeying an order of God, but because of an internal drive to serve God, is a kind of idolatry—and this is so even though the person's intentions are to serve God.

The faith which is expressed in the practical *mitzvot*, in the worship of God, is not something which is meant to give expression or release to man's emotions, but its importance lies in the fact that the person has accepted upon himself what, in the post-biblical tradition, is known as the Yoke of the Kingdom of Heaven and the Yoke of the Torah and *mitzvot*. Faith is expressed in the acts which man does due to his awareness of his obligation to do them, and not because of an internal urge—even when his intention is to worship God, but derives satisfaction for himself through this worship. That is illicit fire. And those that did this, the first priests after Aaron, and did it in the sanctuary, were punished as if they had committed idolatry.

This is a very important lesson for all generations: not to transform the worship of God into a means to release the tensions of one's inner urges, which the person dresses up, possibly with sincerity, as the worship of God.

After this terrible event—where Aaron, who had been anointed as the high priest, was a witness to the fact that his two oldest sons, who had been anointed alongside him, had died here in the sanctuary—even though nothing is said how Aaron felt at that instant, we understand it clearly from what Moses says to him, where he ostensibly comforts him, but with strange words of comfort. Moses tells Aaron that here God's word has been fulfilled, in accordance with what He said, "'I will be sanctified through them that approach Me, and before all the people I will be honored,' and Aaron became silent" (*Vayikra* 10:3). The implication is that, before that, he cried or screamed.

How are we to understand the two parts of this verse? This was a case of *kiddush Hashem*—sanctifying God's name—and the believers in many generations understood it in two different ways.

From one point of view: God's majesty was revealed to the people in the fact that He was sanctified through (or: "by") those that were near to Him; He punished those who were near to Him and had sinned. The sanctification of God's name consisted of the demonstration that God does not play favorites, and does not favor those near to Him. On the contrary—He is more severe with those near Him than with others.

But there is another point of view on "I will be sanctified in them that come nigh Me, and before all the people I will be glorified": the sanctification of God through man. This interpretation refers to the words that "Aaron became silent." This had been a great day of celebration, in which Aaron had been festively anointed to perform the greatest of all activities—to offer the sacrifice of the consecration of the priesthood. Of course, at the moment that his sons died he stopped, but after he heard the words of Moses, "Aaron became silent," and returned to his service. Even though his sons lay dead before him, he was not a mourner, he did not cry. He returned to fulfill his duties.

"I will be sanctified in them that come nigh Me" can be explained that God is sanctified by His deeds among those close to Him; or it can be explained: God is sanctified by the acts that those near Him perform for Him—even at a time when his sons lie dead before him, he performs God's service.

The *sidra* of *Shemini*, after telling us of the great event of the dedication of the sanctuary and the priesthood, deals with a matter which ordered Jewish life throughout the generations—the matter of permitted and forbidden foods, which is the basis for the entire system of kosher and non-kosher foods—this being an integral part of the daily life of observance of the Torah and *mitzvot*. After a discussion of those items which affect man's physical side—the most elementary physical aspect—man's food—we find a concluding and lofty verse which refers to holiness, "For I am God that brought you up out of Egypt, to be your God: you will be holy, for I am holy" (*Vayikra* 11:45). The practical *mitzvot* which a person performs with his body contain a sanctification of God's name.

Here too, there are two very different perceptions regarding the link between "you will be holy" and "for I am holy." There is a profound difference between the "holiness" which refers here to Israel, and "holiness" as it refers to God. In the case of God, holiness is His immanent essence; "Holy" is the attribute of God. Man, though, is not holy, but is commanded to be holy: "you will be holy, for I am holy" (*Vayikra* 11:45). One cannot transfer the concept of holiness, which is the attribute of God, to human reality. Holiness, in the human context, refers only to human duties and functions which are meant to serve God: you will be holy by the fact that you accept upon yourselves the observance of the *mitzvot*. Without them, there can be no holiness, not even for Israel. This is stated clearly in *Sifre* on *Vayikra* 11:45, "You will sanctify yourselves, and you will be holy." "You will sanctify yourselves"—this is the holiness of the *mitzvot*; afterwards, "you will be holy."

As opposed to this is the view that the Jewish people was sanctified by the fact that the Torah was given to it. We will still discuss this viewpoint.

TAZRIA-METZORA

Tazria and *Metzora* are two *sidrot* which deal entirely with the physical side of man in his biological form—both *sidrot* in this sense being a continuation of the second half of the previous *sidra*, *Shemini*, which also deals with man's physical side, his food. *Tazria* and *Metzora* deal with man's sexuality and with plague spots on his body.

Tazria begins immediately with birth, and there we are told that should the child that is born be a son: "On the eighth day the flesh of his foreskin will be circumcised" (*Vayikra* 12:3).

At first glance, we already know of this law of circumcision from Genesis, where it appears as the sublime covenant between God and Abraham—the mark and symbol for all generations, the sign that was embedded in the Jew's body as the covenant of Abraham. Here, though, Maimonides tells us a most surprising thing which has profound significance in terms of faith. Maimonides says that we are not commanded to perform circumcisions because of the covenant with Abraham—that lofty covenant which is described in Genesis—but because of the five Hebrew words in *Tazria*: "On the eighth day the flesh of his foreskin will be circumcised."

What obligates us in terms of faith are only those *mitzvot* which were given at Mount Sinai and thereafter. The worship of God through the *mitzvot* is not a remembrance of ancient times—as claimed by some today who wish to explain their significance as symbolic—that they remind us of ancient times, and who see this as applying especially to circumcision, in which we are reminded of the covenant of Abraham. This idea has penetrated deeply into our religious consciousness, and has been enshrined in formulations: we enter the child on the eighth day "into the covenant of our father Abraham." It is true that we are entering the child into the covenant of our father Abraham, but not because there was a covenant made between Abraham and God—or vice-versa—between God and Abraham—but because we were commanded to enter the child into the covenant of our father Abraham.

The worship of God is not folklore, not even in the most profound sense. It is not a remembrance of that which was, of what happened to the Jewish people and of what happened to our forefathers. The worship of God means fulfilling the commands which were given to us. We fulfill the *mitzva* of circumcision because of the verse, "On the eighth day the flesh of his foreskin will be circumcised."

The major part of this *sidra* deals with the blood of childbirth and that of menstruation, and of ritual impurity and purity—of the biological foulness of human existence. And the *mitzvot* related to this are the worship of God, because the worship of God was imposed on man in that he is human. It was not imposed on man in that he is a spiritual being, but in that he is a physical creature, who must worship God not only with his soul but also with his body—because the body and the soul together are the man.

The Torah does not only deal with the concept with which the *sidra* of *Shemini* concludes, "You will make yourselves holy, and you will be holy" (*Vayikra* 11:45), a verse which might seem to imply that it only relates to matters of one's consciousness and of the spirit; rather, it also deals with what I have referred to as the biological foulness of human existence. This biological foulness is an integral part of natural human reality, and man is commanded to worship God within this reality. That is why the written Torah, as well as the oral Torah, dwells on these matters at length. The order of *Toharot*, which deals with this topic, is the largest of the six orders of the Mishna.

The laws of ritual purity and impurity lapsed for us almost two thousand years ago. Only one item still exists, which is not ritual purity or impurity in that sense: the laws of *nidda* and *tevila*. The laws of *nidda* and *tevila* are not a matter of ritual impurity, but a matter of a religious prohibition imposed upon both the man and woman in their existence as man and woman.

This is analogous to what we find in the *sidra* of *Shemini*—that in his physical activities, in his eating, man must remember that, "I have set God always before me" (*Tehillim* 16:8). He does not just eat, but eats in accordance with the *mitzvot* of God. The same is true with marital relations, this possibly being the most profound of all areas in man's existence in that he is a living creature, where here too man must maintain the awareness that "I have set God always before me." Both man and woman must maintain a specific discipline in their sexual lives, and as this is a discipline that man accepts upon himself only for the reason that he is observing a *mitzva*—which has no other reason—not a social reason, not a hygienic reason, not a moral reason—it is the supreme expression of the worship of God.

One can express this with a different formulation, which appears in the Midrash on the Song of Songs. The Song of Songs, as a text, is devoted entirely to the relationship between man and woman, and God's name is not even mentioned there directly. We know, though, that in our tradition it has become the symbol of the relationship between God and His servants, between God and Israel.

The Midrash refers to one of the verses of the Song of Songs, which, according to its literal meaning is a clearly erotic formulation, "Your belly is like a heap of wheat set about with roses" (*Shir Hashirim* 7:3). The word "set about" has, in the Hebrew, the connotation of "fenced off;" and the Midrash asks: "Since when does one fence off a field with roses?" Doesn't one make a point of fencing it off with thorns or brambles so that people will not enter it? What then is the meaning of "fenced off with roses?" And here the Midrash deals with the most profound relationship in human existence, that between a man and a woman:

> A man longs to see himself under the bridal canopy, because there is no day which is more dear to a man than that, where he will rejoice with his wife. He comes to be with her, and she says to him: "I saw as a rose" (i.e., I saw a drop of menstrual blood). He separates himself from her and she separates herself from him. The one turns his face to this side and the other turns her face to the other side. Who separated them? What snake bit them? Which scorpion harmed them? Which fence is there between them? But these are the words of the Torah, as it states, "You will not approach a woman in her menstrual impurity to have intercourse with her" (*Vayikra* 18:19).

It is because of these words that the two overcome the greatest of desires, on the greatest day, which is meant to supply satisfaction to these desires. That is why it states "fenced off with roses." Roses—a few words in the Torah; not thorns or brambles. That is the highest degree of worshipping God.

ACHAREI MOT-KEDOSHIM

According to this year's Torah reading cycle on *Shabbatot*, the two great s*idrot* of *Acharei Mot* and *Kedoshim* are read together.

I have referred to them as two great *sidrot*. Of course, we are neither authorized nor permitted to give grades to the different *sidrot* of the Torah, yet at the same time we cannot refrain from having a special emotional feeling for these two *sidrot*: *Acharei Mot*, the first part of which deals with the *Yom Kippur* service, and *Kedoshim*, which, as our Sages tell us, is a "*parasha* which includes the majority of the main elements of the Torah," including 53 special *mitzvot*; and the second part of each of these *sidrot*, which deals with the laws related to sexuality, which impose upon this biological, psychological and existential component of our personality a number of safeguards and prohibitions whose significance is nothing less than the acceptance of the Yoke of the Kingdom of Heaven. The term "I am the Lord your God" (or "I am God") recurs 20 times in the two *sidrot*.

A person who has but thirteen minutes to speak on these two *sidrot* may almost throw up his hands at the enormity of the task. I would therefore like to relate here to but a single word, which might indeed be called the key word to these *sidrot*—one might venture to refer to it as an operative term—and that is the term *kedusha*—holiness.

The second *sidra* begins with the powerful verse, "You will be holy: for I the Lord your God am holy" (*Vayikra* 19:2). And in this *sidra* itself, the concept of consecration (or sanctification) of Israel, is mentioned numerous times, "Hallow yourselves therefore, and be holy: for I am the Lord your God. You will keep my statutes, and do them: I am God who makes you holy" (*Vayikra* 20:7–8), and, "And you will be holy to Me: for I God am holy" (*Vayikra* 20:26), and so on.

These are the most elevated commands and goals, yet there are no other verses, expressions and formulations which are more fraught with danger in terms of faith. The problem is that they can be interpreted, and they have been interpreted—sometimes unintentionally, and other times deliberately—as if the Jewish people, by its nature, has something which imparts to it a connotation of sanctity. This view frees the Jew from responsibility, and makes him feel certain in those areas where one may not feel certain, because they are matters which are an aim and a goal and an obligation and a duty, and they are not given automatically. The conversion of the term *kedusha*—as a task and a duty which the Jewish people is obligated to accomplish—to a quality which is innate in the Jewish people—means the conversion of faith to idolatry.

This was already known by the early Sages. When the order of the reading of the *sidrot* was ordained, at which time the different *haftarot* for the *sidrot* were also determined, some *haftarot* were chosen to parallel and complement the *sidra* after which they were read, but in certain cases the *haftara* was specifically assigned against an erroneous and misleading interpretation of the *sidra*. And we see this in the most clear and keen way in these two *sidrot* which deal with the holiness of *Yom Kippur* and the holiness imposed upon the Jewish people.

There are three different *haftarot* for these two *sidrot*, one for each *sidra* when it is read alone, and a third for when the *sidrot* are read together. There are also differences between the Ashkenazic and Sephardic rituals. What is common to all three *haftarot*, though, is the most harsh words of criticism levelled against the way the Jewish people are acting, in comparison to the way they are required to act.

The *haftara* of *Acharei Mot*, which, according to the Ashkenazic ritual, is also read when the two *sidrot* are read together, would seem to be more appropriate for the *sidra* of *Kedoshim*, which begins "You will be holy: for I the Lord your God am holy," where the *haftara* is from *Amos* (9:7), "'Are you not as the Ethiopians to Me, O Israelites?' says God."

It is true that Amos, as do all of the prophets, and especially the Torah itself, notes that when He took them out of Egypt, God separated Israel from the other nations. But the verse which is recited in the *Shema*, "I am the Lord your God, who brought you out of Egypt" (*Devarim* 15:41), has a built-in reservation: "...to be your God." If you do not accept My Godhead, you have no uniqueness. Amos dismisses even this uniqueness, because that in itself is nothing new. After comparing Israel to the Ethiopians, he adds: "Have not I brought up Israel out from Egypt and the Philistines from Caphtor, and the Arameans from Kir?" The fate of all nations in the world is determined by the Master of History. What makes Israel unique is the obligations which it must observe—what was imposed on it, and not what happened to it.

Therefore the prophet Amos can say words which terrify those who consider themselves believers, and who believe in the special choice of the Jewish people, and not in the special task imposed on them: "'The eyes of the Lord God are upon the sinful kingdom, and I will wipe it off the face of the earth; yet I will not utterly destroy the house of Jacob,' says God" (*Amos* 9:8). The house of Jacob exists and will remain as a nation which has the obligation to serve God. But there is no promise that because this obligation was imposed upon it, it is therefore promised the kingdom and is promised the land, even if it does not fulfill its obligation.

The other two *haftarot* which are read with the *sidrot* are chapters in Ezekiel (16 and 23), which are among the harshest rebukes in the Bible. "Cause Jerusalem to know her abominations.... The city sheds blood in its midst.... The chief of Israel, every one of you used power to shed blood.... They disdained father and mother: in the midst of you they have dealt by oppression with the stranger: in you they ill-treated the orphan and the widow…. Informers have worked to procure bloodshed…. In the midst of you they commit lewdness…. They have violated the woman in her period…. One has committed abomination with his neighbor's wife…. You have taken usury and interest…. Her chiefs in their midst are like wolves ravening the prey." And this *haftara* is read alongside the *sidra* of *Kedoshim*: "You will be holy: for I the Lord your God am holy."

These harsh words in Ezekiel are spoken to us. On this very day that I speak to you, I opened my morning newspaper, and found it full of accounts of the murders that have taken place in our midst, and incest and prostitution and lust and rape and theft and armed robbery, and—superfluous to say—idolatry. And yet, there are people that say: "We are by nature a holy people."

We were commanded to be a holy people—and we were not a holy people. And that is what the two *sidrot* with their three *haftarot* indicate.

EMOR

Leviticus has been known in our tradition, since time immemorial, as *Torat Kohanim*, the "Laws of the Priests." The reason for this is obvious, for a great part of it, possibly even most of it, deals with the service in the sanctuary and in the Temple which came thereafter— the laws governing the sacrifices, that being the service of the priests; the very choice of the priests in perpetuity is also enshrined in Leviticus. However, in the more limited and exact sense of the word, *Torat Kohanim* refers to the first half of the *sidra* of *Emor*, which deals with the special obligations and prohibitions pertaining to the priests for all times, none of these applying to anyone who is not of the descendants of Aaron.

This is *Torat Kohanim* in the specific and exact sense of the word, and here too we have a repetition of the key word which we discussed at length last week: the term *kedusha* (commonly translated as "holiness" or "sanctity") and the various forms of words derived from it. In regard to the priests, we are told, "They will be holy to their God...because they present the fire-offerings to God, the food of their God, therefore they will be holy" (*Vayikra* 21:6). And of the individual priest, we are told, "He is holy to his God...he offers the bread of your God: he will be holy to you: for I, God, who hallows you, am holy" (*Vayikra* 21:7–8). And these words are repeated over and over.

And here too, we ask ourselves: Is this holiness—which is specific to the priests and is transferred by inheritance from one generation to the next as descendants of Aaron the priest—something innate in them? Or must we say here as well, that this holiness is only a special obligation imposed upon them? And indeed, the key word to all matters of holiness in *Torat Kohanim* is the term, "to their God"—"They will be holy to their God," and not "they will be holy to you." The Jewish people do not have to treat the priests' status as something which is holy.

This entire concept is discussed with great profundity by one of the latest Torah authorities and thinkers on faith, a few generations before us, *Netziv* of Volozhin, who, in addition to his activities in spreading Torah and ensuring the continued existence of his *yeshiva*, which produced great Torah scholars during the previous two and three generations, also wrote a commentary on the Torah. He notes that the holiness attributed to the priests is conditional on their being holy in their behavior; and they are not holy by nature. They are not to consider themselves as holy, but must regard themselves as obligated to be holy.

He expresses this idea by comparing what the Torah says about the holiness of the priests in our *sidra*, with what we are told about the holiness of the priests in the words of the prophet Ezekiel, possibly 700 or 800 years after the Torah was given—when he portrays the work of the priests in the Temple when it will be rebuilt. We will not go into a discussion here, which may be either historical or midrashic, as to whether Ezekiel was referring to the Second Temple that was constructed in the generation after his, or whether his prophecy referred to the end of days and the aggadic Third Temple.

In any case, in his words about the priests in the Temple which is yet to arise—regardless of whether this refers to the Second Temple which was indeed constructed, or whether it refers to the Third Temple, which exists only as an eschatalogical vision—Ezekiel speaks, among others, on the priestly clothes. The priestly clothes had already been described in the book of Exodus, in the *sidra* of *Tetzaveh*; but here Ezekiel adds a detail, which is not stated specifically in the Torah, "When they [the priests, returning from the sacrificial service in the inner court] go out into the outer court...to the people, they will take off the clothes they wear while serving, and leave them in the holy chambers, and put on other clothes; and they will not imply holiness to the people by their clothes" (*Yechezkel* 44:19).

Netziv explains:

> "They will not imply holiness to the people by their clothes"—this means that they should not appear to the people as holy because of their special priestly clothes. The priestly clothes are meant for serving in the Temple. Outside the Temple, the priests are like any other people, and they should dress as any other person, and should look like any other person. If they do attempt to look holy and special and separate from the people even outside and beyond their work in the Temple, "that is not honoring the name of God, but is arrogance and conceit."

These are the words of *Netziv*. And this applies not only to the priests at the time that the Temple existed, and there was the Divine service and there were priestly clothes, etc., but it applies to all generations. Even if the words of *Netziv* were barbed and aimed at the hasidic rabbis and their antics—his words can be generalized. Those who have special functions related to the service of God—and as we have no Temple and no sacrificial ritual, the functions of serving God today can only be through studying the Torah and teaching the Torah and observing the *mitzvot*—those to whom this applies, or who are accepted as ruling on *halakha*, are only special in terms of this function which they fulfill. Beyond this function, they are as any other man.

This must be said against the spiritual plague, the plague against faith, religion and morals, that has infected, and still infects, certain circles of that part of the Jewish people which accepts the obligation to observe the Torah and the *mitzvot*: to regard certain people as holy in themselves, and not in terms of the function they fill in teaching Torah, and in observing the Torah, and in preserving the Torah. And let it be said: it is nothing but a form of idolatry that has penetrated into Judaism, and is a sign of the withering of faith in God.

Jewish faith does not recognize the concept of holiness except in the context of worshipping God, and does not recognize holiness as an essential part of a person—and one should also add that the same applies to anything which exists in nature or in human reality, in a land or in a building.

"He who distinguishes between holy and secular" is one of the main elements of religious awareness. One is forbidden to raise the secular to the level of the holy, and the secular includes all of man's actions and all of human existence—except for those functions that are intended as an expression of the worship of God.

BEHAR-BECHUKOTAI

Again this year we return to the phenomenon of two *sidrot* which are read together, similar to the case of two weeks ago, when we had the *sidrot* of *Acharei Mot* and *Kedoshim* together. Here we have two large *sidrot*, *Behar* and *Bechukotai*, and both are so important that again I found it difficult to say something of value in the few minutes at my disposal.

Behar is the *sidra* that deals with *shemitta*—the sabbatical year—and *yovel*—the jubilee year, where we have social and economic rules of society as ordained by the Torah; the land returning to its original owners, slaves being freed, and if we go into this somewhat more in depth—in reality, the abolishing of private ownership of land in the Land of Israel. By Torah law, a person who owns land becomes nothing but a renter—he has rented the land from the Lord, God of heaven and earth, for fifty years.

This regime, and there is doubt if it was ever observed in full, is a powerful program for arranging social reality according to the Torah.

The beginning of the *sidra Bechukotai* is the great blessing to the Jewish people if it observes the Torah, but this is followed by the *tokhecha*—the admonition and curse—with 49 verses which warn of the destruction of the land, the destruction of the nation, and exile, for the sin of violating the Torah's laws. The admonition, which was said in the Sinai desert by Moses as he received it from God, is repeated in an even more concise and forceful manner by Moses about forty years later, before his death.

The common element in the two admonitions is that there is no promise of redemption to follow. The promise of redemption after the destruction and after the exile is given in the Torah in a different place, in the *sidra* of *Nitzavim*, where the return—"the Lord your God will restore you from your captivity"—is dependent on repentance—"When (or: "if") you will return to your God" (*Devarim* 30:2). But the rebuke in our *sidra*, similar to the rebuke in the *sidra* of *Ki Tavo*, does not state that the redemption will surely come. As opposed to this, there are two vital segments here, whose meaning in terms of faith is almost beyond almost anything else in terms of understanding the relationship or link between Israel and its God.

After warning of the destruction and the exile, we are told, "I will remember My covenant with Jacob, and also My covenant with Isaac, and also My covenant with Abraham will I remember; and I will remember the land" (*Vayikra* 26:42). Also, in regard to the exile, it states, "And yet for all that, when they are in the land of their enemies, I will not cast them away, neither will I abhor them, to destroy them utterly, and to break my covenant with them: for I am the Lord their God. On their behalf I will remember the covenant of the ancients, whom I brought out of Egypt in the sight of the nations, that I might be their God: I am God" (*Vayikra* 26:44–45).

These verses, which are most striking, are ones that generation after generation of the Jewish people looked toward. Let us examine what they say: they state that God remembers the covenant, but there is not the slightest hint of what will happen. The covenant is remembered by God: "He remembers the covenant." These verses serve as a basis for a deeply held popular belief, also shared by many deep religious thinkers, that we—the Jewish people—may rely on the merits of our forefathers: "I will remember My covenant with Jacob, and also My covenant with Isaac, and also My covenant with Abraham will I remember; and I will remember the land"—the merits of our forefathers stand us in good stead.

But all those who are dependent on this ignore the fact that our Sages, who knew the Torah and knew all these verses, deliberated on the question: "When were the merits of the forefathers exhausted?" This same discussion is repeated in the Midrash on the verse, "I will remember the covenant of the ancients": "Until when were the merits of the forefathers valid?" And it is the opinion of the greatest *Amora'im* that the merits of the forefathers have already been exhausted. It was through the merits of our forefathers that we took the Land of Cana'an, and it was through our sins that we lost it.

Nine hundred or a thousand years after these discussions among the greatest *Amora'im*, the same question was raised in *Tosafot*—at a time when the Talmud had already been in existence for hundreds of years, and the *Ba'alei HaTosafot* knew it and the world of later *midrashim*. They also knew all the religious beliefs prevalent among the Jewish people—and they too, *Tosafot*, took it as given: the merits of the forefathers have been exhausted. There is one of the greatest among *Ba'alei HaTosafot*, though, *Rabbenu Tam*, who indicates that even though the merits of the forefathers have been exhausted, the covenant with the forefathers has not been nullified, and it is this that the Torah tells us is still in effect.

The term "covenant" can be explained in two ways. In the *sidra* of *Noach*, after the flood, God makes a covenant that the flood will not recur, and the rainbow in the sky is the sign of that covenant, a sign that the natural order of things will not change. It is clear that in this case, the covenant is a promise by God. Nature itself is not obligated to do anything, and cannot assume any obligation of any kind.

But there is a covenant which is bilateral, where each side assumes obligations toward the other party to the covenant. Here we understand that *Rabbenu Tam* understood the term "the covenant" in this second sense. A covenant between Israel and its God, or, possibly, between the God of Israel and His nation, still exists because one of the parties is "He who remembers the covenant." But whether the covenant will be executed depends on the second party as well.

The Torah—when it tells us of the great promise: "I will remember My covenant," and that even when we are in the land of our enemies the covenant is not forgotten by God—does not promise us redemption, because there is no merit to warrant this. For the covenant, which exists in potential, to also have actual results, the other party to the covenant must act. And the other party is the Jewish people.

This too must be said against that idolatrous faith which is prevalent even among the community which regards itself as having faith in God and His Torah: that we are unconditionally guaranteed redemption. There is a clear midrashic statement: "Three things were given conditionally—the Land of Israel, the Temple, and the kingship of the house of David." Only the Torah and the priesthood were given unconditionally.

CHUMASH

BAMIDBAR

BAMIDBAR

The contents of the *sidra* of *Bamidbar* deal with administrative, demographic and statistical matters related to administration and management, the organization of the nation into its different divisions and tribes, the way the camp was set up, and afterwards, again—the special administrative arrangements for the tribe of Levi, its division into families, the assignment of duties within the sanctuary among these families, and their appointment to the sanctuary service. This *sidra* includes a census of 600,000 people, and I believe that I would not be wrong if I say that this is the first census recorded in history.

All these topics seem to refer to the time that Israel was in the desert and to the different arrangements involved in the trip to the Land of Cana'an. But the *sidra* has a *haftara*, and it is with this remarkable *haftara* that I would like to deal within the limited time available to us.

The *haftara*, chapter 2 of Hosea, was appended to the *sidra* of *Bamidbar* for what appears to be no more than a formal reason. As I mentioned, the *sidra* includes a census of the population, and the chapter in Hosea begins with the words, "The number of the Israelites will be as the sand of the sea"—a great destiny.

But the main content of that chapter in Hosea is the *brit*—covenant—between God and His nation Israel, or, we may say, between Israel and its God, an issue not dealt with in this *sidra* at all, but dealt with at length in the previous *sidra*. I would therefore like to discuss this *haftara* as the continuation and explanation of what I stated last week on the *sidra* of *Bechukotai*.

The *sidra* of *Bechukotai* contains the great and terrible admonition and the message of destruction and exile. Yet this great admonition ends with something most exalted, which was part of the faith of generations of Jews: "Then will I remember My *brit* with Jacob, and also My *brit* with Isaac, and also My *brit* with Abraham will I remember; and I will remember the land.... I will on their behalf remember the *brit* of the ancients, whom I brought out of Egypt in the sight of the nations, that I might be their God" (*Vayikra* 26:42, 45). I have already noted that there is no word there on what will happen or occur objectively. What we are told is a powerful and great message: the *brit* between God and His nation, and between Israel and its God, still stands before God; but *brit* is a two-way relation, therefore it will only move from potential to actuality if the other side, namely the Jewish people, fulfills its obligations.

Chapter 2 of Hosea deals entirely with this *brit*, and in a most moving manner. It describes the relationship between God and Israel as that between a man and a woman, as a marriage covenant. It describes it in terms which remind us of the Song of Songs, which, according to our tradition, is also an allegory for the relationship between God and Israel, and speaks of the breach of the covenant by Israel. The description of the renewal of this covenant in the future is also most moving, and concludes with two lofty verses, "I will betroth you to Me forever; I will betroth you to Me in righteousness, and in justice, and in tenderness, and in mercy. I will betroth you to Me in faithfulness: and you will know God" (*Hoshea* 2:21–22).

"I will betroth you"—the betrothal is between God and Israel, and it stems from the righteousness and the justice and the tenderness and the mercy, which are all descriptions of the Divine. (I will not deal here with the major issue of the meaning of attributes of the Godhead.)

"I will betroth you to Me is faithfulness"—one should note that the term *emuna* (translated here as faithfulness) in the Bible, everywhere, does not have the meaning of the word *emuna* as commonly used in late and contemporary Hebrew, namely faith, especially religious faith. The meaning of *emuna* in the Bible is always "faithfulness," and here it means the faithfulness of the betrothed to one another.

But afterwards there are three Hebrew words which are crucial: "You will know God." Righteousness and justice and tenderness and mercy and faithfulness all pertain to God, and they are eternal; they are eternal and are not dependent on the circumstances or on man's behavior. But for the betrothal to be valid, it is essential that the basic condition exists: "You will know God." Knowing God is the one condition for the renewal of the covenant, and without it the covenant remains only potential, but is not actualized.

And this reminds us of the words of the prophet who lived about 150 years after Hosea, the words of Jeremiah, "Let any man boast only of this, that he understands and knows Me, that I am God who exercises kindness (or: "love"), justice and righteousness (these seem to be the best of the various translations of the three great biblical Hebrew terms, *chesed*, *mishpat* and *tzedaka*) in the world" (*Yirmiyahu* 9:24). There is an analogy here: God shows tenderness and justice and mercy, and in Hosea—"I will betroth you to Me in righteousness, and in justice, and in tenderness, and in mercy," but with the proviso that "man understands and knows Me, that I am God who exercises tenderness and justice and mercy in the world" (*Yirmiyahu* 9:23).

God exercises tenderness and justice and mercy whether man knows it or not, but only if man knows and understands God does this have meaning in reality. Similarly, "I will betroth you to Me in righteousness, and in judgment, and in lovingkindness, and in mercy. I will betroth you to Me in faithfulness"—provided that "you will know God." The covenant between Israel and its God, as something which is fulfilled in reality, depends on the Jewish people.

NASO

In our talk on the longest *sidra* in the Torah, a *sidra* which deals with numerous topics, we will devote the time available to us to discuss but a single verse, and we may be more specific—to two Hebrew words within that verse, because the understanding of these words and the verse within which they appear deals with profound and significant assumptions and reflections regarding the problems of belief in Divine revelation, the nature of Divine revelation, and God's speaking to man.

After the long *parasha* of the dedication of the sanctuary, when it was consecrated for its assigned purpose to serve as the Tent of Assembly—the place where Moses would convene with the *Shekhina* in order to receive the Torah, to hear the word of God and then to pass it on to Israel—we are told in the last verse of this long *sidra*: "When Moses entered the Tent of Assembly to speak with Him, he heard the voice speaking (and the Hebrew original uses an unusual grammatical construct of the verb "to speak") to him from above the cover over the ark of testimony, from between the two cherubs: and He spoke to him" (*Bamidbar* 7:89).

God's speech—God speaking to man, or to a prophet where the word of God is received by the prophet—is expressed twice in this verse, in two different grammatical forms: at the end of the verse in the usual form, "and He spoke (*medaber*) to him" (the form "God spoke to Moses" appears scores of times in the Torah; "the word of God was to" a certain prophet—appears frequently in the books of the Prophets). But before this, it states, "*middaber*." Was it not for the vocalization which we owe to the *masora*, and if we had in front of us only the text as written in the Torah scroll, where there are no vowels, we almost certainly would have read the verse automatically as "he heard the voice speaking (in Hebrew *medaber*) to him." Here, though, it states "*middaber*"—this is not the *pi'el* (active) form of the verb, but the *hitpa'el* (reflexive) form, indicating an action which reflects back to the person who performs it.

What is the meaning of *middaber*? (One should note that this form of the conjugation of the Hebrew root "DBR" appears in only one other place in the Bible, that being Ezekiel's vision of the Divine Chariot.)

On this verse, *Rashi* states: "'*middaber*' is like '*mitdaber*' [i.e., the reflexive form]. It is respect for God to say here that He was speaking to Himself, and Moses heard from his inner self." In other words, when the Torah states "*middaber* to him," the words "to him" really mean "to Himself." Moses heard God speaking to Himself, and Moses heard from his inner self. This was not an acoustic event, in which the sound reached Moses, but there was a process in Moses' self-awareness, whereby, in the bold words of *Rashi*, he heard God speaking to Himself. He became aware what was happening in the Godhead. He understood God's meaning, and he heard God's voice from within his own self.

Rashi's interpretation is surprising, and almost astounding. *Rashi* lived two generations before Maimonides, but in these few words *Rashi* gives Maimonides' entire view on prophecy. *Rashi* parallels closely the view of Maimonides, who clearly, and with great conceptual profundity, presents prophecy as something which occurs in the self-awareness of the man who has reached the ultimate degree given to man in perceiving God. We are not surprised at Maimonides, for this view of prophecy is in keeping with his entire system of faith. But *Rashi*, who is always considered to be of naive faith and far from philosophic thought and analysis, says the exact same thing. This must indicate that this view reflects something of basic faith, and is not an expression of the introduction of alien

philosophical concepts into the world of Judaism. The speech of
God to man signifies that man perceives God.

A very interesting question is how *Rashi* reached this conclusion.
We do not find this idea in any religious source before *Rashi*—
neither in the *halakha* nor even in the Aggada or Midrash. What is
most interesting is that our two ancient *Targumim*, Onkelos and
Yehonatan, do not note anything unusual about the text: they translate the text here (*middaber*) using the identical word they do for the
latter, common reference (*vayedaber*). The same is true for the
Septuagint, which preceded the two *Targumim*, and which uses the
same Greek word for both Hebrew words.

But in our case, and about 400 years after *Rashi*, one of the Torah
commentators, who is also considered to be one of our classic
commentators, quotes *Rashi* and formulates his words in a very
profound philosophic form, and this is what R. Ovadya Seforno
says:

> "*middaber eilav*—speaking to Himself" (the same words as are used by
> *Rashi*)—"for God does everything for Himself" (*Mishlei* 16:4), and by
> knowing Himself, He knows and does good to others, and the action
> manifests itself to the one affected by God in accordance with his capa-
> bility, and he (i.e., *Rashi*) explains the meaning of every "saying" in the
> Torah, where it states, "and God spoke."

One should note that one of the Christian translators—namely
Luther—also understood these words in this form, whereas many of
the Jewish commentators did not understand it in this way. Luther,
in an unequivocal form (in German, there is no doubt what he
meant), explains the word *middaber eilav* as "*redend zu sich*"—
"speaking to Himself," while the later reference of *vayedaber* is
translated by him as "*Er redete zu ihm*"—"He spoke to him." Here it
is appropriate to ask from where Luther derived this: did he know,
directly or indirectly, of what *Rashi* had said?

In any event, when the Torah states "the voice *middaber* to him," as explained by *Rashi*, and explained afterwards by Seforno, we find a very important principle of faith and of understanding the meaning of God's speaking to man.

BEHA'ALOTEKHA

The *sidra* of *Beha'alotekha* contains numerous topics. It contains many *mitzvot*, some of which refer to the service in the sanctuary and some which are for all times, but it also contains the story of events that occurred in the desert, some of great importance in regard to the organization of Israel and the internal arrangements among Israel, and some of them details of events, including the famous incident (which we do not understand completely) of what happened between Miriam and Aaron and their brother Moses. It is within the framework of that story that we find a comment about Moses which is extremely well-known: "The man Moses was very humble (more), than any man on earth."

A number of the earlier and later rabbis have noted that we know of Moses from his deeds: the first redeemer of Israel and its legislator, through whom the Torah was given to Israel, and who performed the miracles and wonders. In accordance with these actions, we can come to appreciate his personality, but the Torah does not specifically describe his character, except for this one time, in which it specifically notes one of his characteristics.

No place in the Torah does it state specifically that Moses was wiser than any man, nor does it say that he was more righteous than any man, nor does it say that he was mightier than any man, even though we can deduce from events that he was wise, with the greatest comprehension of any man, and that he was righteous and mighty. But the Torah finds it proper, or necessary, to stress only one thing: that Moses was more humble than any other man. And this gives us much food for thought.

Humility, without any doubt, is a high level of human perfection. Human nature is such that each person considers himself to be great and important—if not consciously, at least subconsciously. In other words, it is not natural for a person to be humble.

But there are humble people. And the humbleness found among people of a high ethical and intellectual character can be the product of one of two reasons: either they, by self-criticism, recognize their faults and weaknesses, or they overcome man's nature of venerating himself, boasting and praising himself, and they appear as humble. Here we are not referring to hypocrisy. These are people who overcome those feelings of superiority, pride and importance that a person normally ascribes to himself, and they are humble.

But in regard to Moses we are told, "The man Moses was very humble (more), than any man on the face of the earth." In which way was he humble? Moses was the man who reached the highest comprehension of God that any man is able to attain; this is agreed to by all thinkers on faith in the Jewish world. One might then have imagined that if a person attains that high a level, it will be impossible for him not to be aware of the level he has attained. Furthermore, we find one of the greatest prophets of Israel who arose 700 or 800 years after Moses, Jeremiah, who states, "let him that boasts boast of this, that he understands and knows Me, that I am God...." (*Yirmiyahu* 9:22). In other words, a person may boast of his knowledge of God—not of his knowledge in general, and not of his might, and not of his wealth, but of his knowledge of God.

Jeremiah was one of the prophets that arose among Israel, and Moses was the chief of the prophets. He attained a comprehension of God which was superior to that of any of the other prophets. On this, the Talmud states, "All the prophets looked through a dark glass, and our teacher Moses looked through a clear glass." It is only one who attains the level of Moses, and who really "understands and knows God," that really realizes that no man can understand and know God. He attains the truest and greatest humility.

In the case of a prophet—his perception tells him that he compre-
hends God, and therefore he has reason to exult. But if a person
attains the level of Moses—of whom we are told that God spoke to
him "face to face," and that "in all My house he is faithful," or, at
the end of the Torah, "that God knew him face to face"—one who
has attained this level is able to realize and understand that, in the
most profound meaning of the issue, man cannot comprehend God
because God is beyond human comprehension.

And that is the highest level of humbleness, which only Moses
was able to attain. On that comment by the Sages, *Rashi* states few
but keen words: "all the prophets looked through a dark glass, and
our teacher Moses looked through a clear glass"—"All the prophets
looked through a dark glass—and thought that they saw, and our
teacher Moses looked through a clear glass [in other words, he, one
might imagine, was able to see God]—and knew that he had not
seen Him to His face."

SHELACH LEKHA

The *sidra* of *Shelach Lekha* is famous for its account of the spies, the event which involved the grave crisis of the exodus of the people who left Egypt, as a result of which the generation was sentenced to die in the desert. The memory of that episode has reverberated throughout Jewish history to the extent that at a later period, the night that the people cried after hearing the spies' tale was identified with, "She weeps in the night" (*Eikha* 1:2)—the night of *Tisha B'Av*.

But we will not deal with this, nor will we deal with the two subsequent sections which concern the laws related to coming to Cana'an and the sacrificial ritual. All three of these sections concerned only that period, and we will devote our talk to the short section which concludes the *sidra*, a *parasha* of but five verses—the *parasha* of *tzitzit*, which is relevant to all generations, the law of which continues to be observed by hundreds of thousands of Jews who say the *Shema* each day.

Nor will we discuss here the actual *mitzva* of *tzitzit*, regarding which our Sages make the astonishing statement that "the *mitzva* of *tzitzit* is equivalent to all the other *mitzvot* together." There are more than half a dozen—I believe seven or eight—*mitzvot* about which our Sages used the eloquent and hyperbolic statement that "this *mitzva* is equivalent to all the other *mitzvot* together." We are not surprised that this statement is used in regard to the *mitzva* of circumcision, which is the token of the covenant; nor that it is stated about *Shabbat*, which is also a sign, or on the duty of *Talmud Torah*, which is the Jew's participation in the Torah; but it is surprising that this statement is made about the relatively minor *mitzva* of *tzitzit*.

It is possible to discuss or study this, but we will not do so either. Instead, we will concentrate on one of these five verses. The *tzitzit* are both a sign and a remembrance, or, in other words, they are meant to remind man of something: "You will not go astray after your heart and your eyes" (*Bamidbar* 15:39).

It is clear that the eyes mentioned in the verse here are not the eyes one uses for physical vision, but are spiritual eyes, the eyes which understand and recognize things. Nor is the heart the anatomic heart, but it is our drives, the mental factors, which are present within man. The meaning of the verse would therefore appear to be clear. But here we can ask: if it is not the eyes—namely what a person sees and recognizes in reality, nor the heart—his internal drives—which should direct him, then what should direct him?

Here we have the opportunity to look into one of the major issues of religious thought and moral thought in general: the relationship between religious faith and a moral position. We know that there are many people who attempt to strip religion of its religious content and limit it to ethics, and who explain the Torah as a study text for the moral perfection of man. But here comes this verse toward the end of the *Shema*, and teaches us something.

The Hebrew word *mussar*, which is currently used to mean ethics, has only been used to mean this relatively recently, but in the Bible, the word has an entirely different meaning. The concept of ethics/*mussar* is understood by many as a certain program of human behavior, "moral behavior." There is no greater error than this. *Mussar* is not a program of behavior, but a program of what a person's intentions and goals should be. All human behavior, every action a person takes, is, as an action, morally neutral.

Note the following: take two cases where a person cocks a gun and pulls the trigger while aiming at another person, whom he kills. In both cases, we have the identical action, and yet in the one case, the person may be considered to be a base murderer, and in the other, his action may be considered to be a heroic act, even one of self-sacrifice, where the person seeks to protect his wife, children, etc. Thus we see that we do not judge the act in itself, but the intention behind the act. Ethical theory gives a person guidelines as to his volition: what his intentions must be. The ethical person is the person whose intentions are good and correct. But here the question immediately arises: What are good and correct intentions, and what makes a particular decision a moral one?

In the history of philosophical thought on ethics, various answers have been given, and I will relate to two of them, which appear to me to be the most significant ones.

One answer is that the moral decision of man is expressed in the fact that the person must focus his desires not on his own interests, not on improving his condition in the world and in solving his own problems, but must focus them in accordance with his recognition and understanding of the great truth of the overall reality, of which he is a part; or, in other words: as the person sees and understands the world. This was the answer by one of the great men—possibly, in terms of character, the greatest person—in western thought: Socrates. It is on this that the Greek ethical theory of the Stoa is based, and in the new era—the ethical theory of Spinoza.

The second answer is that man's ethical decision lies in focusing his desires not on the world as it is, or as he understands and recognizes the world, but as he recognizes himself, his duty, or, in the words of the great man that stated this: "the moral law which is within us." This, of course, is the answer of Kant, the greatest thinker on ethical theory in modern philosophy.

And here we come back to our verse, "You will not go astray after your heart"—this is a negation of Kant's principle; "do not go astray after your eyes"—this is a negation of Socrates' principle; and the reason for this is given immediately: "I am your God." All ethical decisions, whether those of Socrates or those of Kant, stem from the fact that man regards himself as standing before his fellow-man: how a person relates to his fellow-man is his ethical decision. Religious faith, on the other hand, is based on the fact that man sees himself as standing before God, and carrying out his obligations to

God is what guides him. It is therefore possible that an act carried out in accordance with an ethical decision, and the same act carried out in accordance with a religious decision, will be different actions, because their intent is different. Performing a *mitzva* of the Torah is not an ethical act but an act of religious faith, and that is the meaning of "You will not go astray after your heart and your eyes…. I am the Lord your God." The recognition of "I am the Lord your God" removes man from the realm of human values, and places him in the realm of the relationship between man and his God.

KORACH

The *sidra* of *Korach* follows that of *Shelach*, whose last *parasha*—which directly precedes *Korach*, is that of *tzitzit*, which we discussed last week.

It would appear that there is no link between the last *parasha* of *Shelach* and the first one of *Korach*, even though they are consecutive in the Torah. One may, though, be able to say that the affair of *Korach* is linked to the affair of the spies, which precedes the *parasha* of *tzitzit* in the Torah—for both with the spies and with *Korach*, we find a revolt against Moses' leadership; although according to the way they appear in the Torah, the *parasha* of *Korach* follows after that of *tzitzit*. We will not get involved here in the famous discussion as to whether the Torah is arranged chronologically or not. In any event, in the text the two are consecutive.

Yet one is able to find that even though the two topics seem to be worlds apart, there is a close link between them, in terms of the key word which appear in both. And the distance between the two appearances of the key word is but a few verses.

The conclusion of the *parasha* of *tzitzit*, which is also the end of the *Shema*, is something which every Jew who says the *Shema* daily knows by heart, "That you may remember, and do all My *mitzvot*, and be holy to your God. I am the Lord your God, who brought you out of Egypt, to be your God: I am your God" (*Bamidbar* 15:40–41). Immediately after this, we read, "Korach, the son of Izhar, the son of Kehat, the son of Levi, and Dathan and Abiram, the sons of Eliav, and On, the son of Pelet, sons of Reuben, took...." (*Bamidbar* 16:1), and in this they were joined by another 250 notables. Now what did they take? They took up rebellion against Moses and his leadership, and the words ascribed to them as a complaint against Moses are: "for all the community, all of them are holy."

The difference between the holiness mentioned in the verse on *tzitzit* and that in regard to Korach is the difference between faith in God and idolatry. The holiness mentioned in the verse on *tzitzit* is not a fact, but a goal. There we are not told, "You are holy," but rather there is a demand (a demand which it is doubtful that any person can meet, but each one must be aware that it is demanded of him): "You are to be holy." In Korach's view, though, "all the community, all of them are holy": holiness is something granted to us; we are holy.

The difference between the two is most profound. On the one hand—in the *parasha* of *tzitzit*—holiness is expressed as the most lofty state that can be attained through man's decisions on religious faith; he is required to demand this goal of himself. He is not promised anything, nothing is granted him—but demands are made of him. And the believer sees this as a great privilege given him over those upon whom this task was not imposed. On the other hand, we have holiness according to Korach and his adherents, which is something base and disreputable: in essence, the person absolves himself of responsibility, of the mission imposed upon him and of the obligation to exert himself; he is smugly sure that he is already holy. And we have been aware of this at all times—that even the most contemptible person can boast that he is a member of a holy nation.

But one should note, without distorting the fact, that in the long history of the Jewish awareness of Judaism, these two concepts of holiness have existed side by side. There is no doubt that it is from the holiness mentioned in the verse in the *parasha* of *tzitzit*, which is said by Jews in the *Shema* each day, that the entire world of laws which obligate man, the entire world of *halakha*, developed, for these laws are but an expression of the fact that the person strives to cleave to God by directing his behavior, not according to his natural proclivities, but rather according to what he sees as obligations imposed upon him by God in accordance with the Torah. But the fact remains that there were believers, sincere believers, in every generation, who believed in a holiness which is inherent in the Jewish people—because it is the Jewish people, and not because that people performs a certain task. Had we wanted to phrase this cynically, we could have noted that after being told that Korach and his followers were swallowed up by the ground, we are told in another text, "the sons of Korach did not die" (*Bamidbar* 16:1). The Korachites exist to this very day—these are the people whose religious faith is expressed in their reliance on the holiness granted to the Jewish people, whose descendants they are, and they feel they are already at that level which man is commanded in the *Shema* to attempt to attain.

I would like to quote here the words of a contemporary Torah scholar and believer, who did not say anything innovative in this regard, but formulated it marvelously, this being R. Yaakov Moshe Harlap, one of the rabbis of Jerusalem and a disciple of R. Avraham Yitzchak Kook. R. Harlap, in a commentary he wrote on the Eight Chapters of Maimonides, stresses this idea:

What is the most important thing in man's reality? For R. Harlap, man's reality is, of course, his standing before God: Is it what man achieves, or the efforts that go into achieving it? R. Harlap, based on ideas he finds in Maimonides, which he explains, states that the main thing is the effort man puts into achieving something, and on this he adds a very interesting comment indeed. The value of the effort is not dependent on whether the thing is achieved or not; not only that, but it is possible that a person may be aware that he will never be able to achieve this goal, but the effort which he puts into trying to achieve it is the supreme value. That is what is meant by, "That you may remember, and do all My *mitzvot*, and be holy." It is possible that the condition that the Torah makes for man's being holy, "That you may remember, and do all My *mitzvot*" is beyond his nature, but man is nevertheless commanded to attempt to fulfill it—to attempt to be holy.

And on the other hand, there is the Korachite view of a holiness implicit in the Jewish people, a view which also has been held by some of the great believers. We find something along these lines in the spiritual world of R. Yehudah Halevi in his *Kuzari* (this is not found in R. Yehudah Halevi's prayers and *selichot*, but there is something like it in his *Kuzari*—"all the community, all of them are holy," in Korach's sense); the same is true with *Maharal* of Prague, and, closer to our generation—in the thought of Rav Kook, who forgot the important topic of "who separates between holy and profane," and sought and found holiness in the very existence of the Jewish people, and thereby led astray his disciples and the disciples of his disciples, both spiritually and in their actions.

From this, we see that there is a vast difference between the holiness of the end of the *Shema* and the holiness in the story of Korach and his cohorts, who were evidently not swallowed up in the ground, and still live to this very day.

CHUKKAT

The first *parasha* in the *sidra* of *Chukkat* is one of the most baffling in the Torah—the *mitzva* of the red heifer, which, over the generations, has been explained by every possible method of Torah interpretation: *peshat*, *remez*, *derash* and *sod*. We will not deal with it here.

Afterwards, most of the *sidra* deals with a great period of our history, described very briefly here, but relating to the period of 38 of the 40 years the Israelites spent in the desert: from the great crisis of the episode with the spies, in the second year after the Israelites left Egypt, until the time they first began to enter Cana'an, at the beginning of the 40th year, and the beginning of the conquest of the land—the taking of Transjordan, which became the inheritance of two and a half tribes.

In this long historical span, which is given in only the most brief of outlines, there was one event which, in terms of its spiritual and religious significance and content, is astonishing and disturbing: the decree that Moses—Israel's first redeemer (as he is known in our tradition), the faithful shepherd of Israel, the "man of God" and the "servant of God," who was charged with the task of taking Israel out of Egypt and receiving the Torah and then bringing Israel to the promised land—was not to enter the land, and would die in the desert. And, as we see from the end of the Torah, Moses was not even buried in the soil of the Land of Israel.

This episode is known in our tradition as "the sin of Moses"—and we are astounded. And when I say "we," I also include past generations, who studied the Torah and delved into it and pondered over it.

God spoke to both Moses and Aaron in the most severe fashion, "You were unfaithful to Me," "You did not uphold My sanctity" (*Devarim* 32:51)—and that was why God decreed that they would die outside Cana'an. And we ask: "How did Moses break faith with God? What was his sin? How did he not uphold God's sanctity?"

These matters are not explained in the Torah. Those who studied and delved into the Torah raised many and varied hypotheses in attempting to find the meaning from the text itself, and could not find any. Various hypotheses have been offered over the generations by commentators and thinkers, and one may say that none of them is satisfactory.

Among the purely formal explanations are those that Moses was commanded to speak to the rock, and instead hit it; or rather than instead of hitting it once, he hit it twice. It is superfluous to note that that doesn't explain Moses "breaking faith" or his "not upholding God's sanctity," and it certainly does not explain the punishment. Even Maimonides, when he (incidentally) relates to this episode, offers a hypothesis that Moses was punished because of a flaw that was revealed here in his character: he became angry when he turned to the people with the words: "Hear now, you rebels" (*Devarim* 32:51), where his anger was out of place. However Maimonides himself brings his hypothesis with certain reservations as to whether this is indeed the correct interpretation.

But it is possible that this event has a more profound explanation. In any event, a midrashic source states it—and I would like to relate to this. In order for us to understand the significance of the interpretation, we must realize one fact that is possibly decisive in every attempt to understand the affair: the fact that Moses himself is not aware that he sinned. On every occasion—and this is repeated three times in the Torah—when Moses pleads to God to annul His decree and to allow him to achieve the goal for which he worked for forty years—he never asks God for forgiveness for his sin, but merely asks for the decree to be annulled. And hundreds of years later, in the historical consciousness of the Jewish people, in that great chapter in Psalms which summarizes the history of the exodus from Egypt, we are only told, "They angered him also at the waters of strife and Moses suffered because of them" (*Tehillim* 106:32). It was not Moses that did evil, but he was punished because of the sins of Israel. Thus we ask: Did Moses sin or did he not sin? If Moses, the most humble of all men, was not cognizant of having sinned, who are we to seek for sins in Moses? And why this decree against him?

And yet, in that same Midrash, we are told that God said to Moses in regard to his prayers for the decree to be annulled: "Moses, with what do you wish to enter the land?" The Midrash wishes to say, and explains it this way later: the generation that you led was not granted the privilege of entering the land—and you, the leader of that generation, wish to enter? This is analogous to a shepherd whose flock was torn to shreds by wild animals—can he then say: "I'm going home now"? In other words, the leader has a share in the sins of his generation, for the sins which were committed under his leadership, even if he himself is not—either legally or morally, or by any other human criterion—responsible for the sins, the omissions, or the errors of those under him. Yet he has a share in their sins.

This idea, which is expressed most clearly in the case of Moses, is also known among other nations: the leader shares in every error, in every sin by negligence, and in every deliberate sin that took place under his leadership. Among sailors, there used to be a concept of honor, that the captain of a foundering ship would not attempt to save himself if there was still anyone left on board that needed to be saved; the captain had to perish with the ship. And in modern-day concepts, in the social and political spheres, we refer to this as the assumption of ministerial responsibility, and the fate of Moses illustrates this in a paradigmatic way.

But this is something we are lacking. And that says something about the quality of our leaders. We have reached the stage of being led by people without any self-respect, leaders who attempt to save themselves at the expense of the sins, omissions and errors made by those under them, who acted under their leadership. This is unlike the faithful shepherd that the Jewish people had, who, when the people died as a result of their sins, died with them, even though there was no sin on his part.

BALAK

The *sidra* of *Balak*, which is known as the affair of Balaam, is one of the astonishing *sidrot* of the Torah. The narrative of the event and its central character, Balaam, is puzzling. Who was this man, whose curse posed a great danger for those whom he cursed, and whose words later turned into a blessing—and who foresaw the greatness of Israel in the end of days? Who was the man that caused a great calamity to Israel, and who was finally killed for this by Israel?

One should note the fact that Balaam is never referred to in the Bible as a prophet, but whenever the Torah speaks of his essence—which it does twice—he is referred as Balaam the magician. As far as the Torah is concerned, the practice of magic is proscribed and despicable; yet Balaam merits God appearing to him, and he even testifies that he "sees visions of God."

The ancient rabbis were astonished at this, and this astonishment continues among those who study the Torah to this day. And a measure of bewilderment is also visible in a statement by the Sages, that, at first, seems to really be staggering. On the verse at the end of the Torah, "There arose no more a prophet in Israel like Moses, whom God knew face to face" (*Devarim* 34:10), one of the *Amora'im* states: "In Israel none arose, but among the Gentiles one did arise. And who was that? Balaam son of Be'or."

It is unthinkable that the author of this statement wished to place Balaam on the same level as Moses. One should understand the statement, and a number of commentators on the Torah have already suggested this, as indicating that the Gentiles had someone whose function, in regard to those nations, paralleled that of Moses in

Israel. Moses was Israel's legislator, and the Gentiles also had a person who was their legislator—and this is no indication whatsoever of a comparison of the rank of the one with the other.

But we immediately ask ourselves: Was Balaam then a legislator for the Gentiles? Did he parallel Moses, Israel's legislator? There is no hint at this anywhere in the Torah. He was a magician, and the Gentiles believed in his magic powers, but where do we see that he exercised the function of a legislator, of one who laid down religious principles, etc., as Moses did? We are immediately forced to think of someone who, while of Jewish descent, nevertheless fulfilled the same function for the Gentiles as Moses did for Israel, and who became—whether with his compliance or without it, intentionally or not—the one who laid down the basis for their faith. And that person was Jesus.

The strange association between Balaam, son of Be'or, and Jesus, who lived about 1,500 years after him, is a common theme in the talmudic and midrashic literature, and is expressed in various ways. Sometimes, Balaam is portrayed as a true prophet to the Gentiles, who speaks to them in God's name, and warns them of Jesus who will arise in the future. That is the way it is in *Midrash Tanchuma* (and this statement, of course, only appears in uncensored printings), in regard to the words of Balaam in his blessing of Israel, "God is not a man that He should lie" (*Bamidbar* 23:19). This is the language of the Midrash:

> Balaam foresaw [here he is really foreseeing the future], that a man, born of woman [a clear reference to the Christian mythology] would arise, who would proclaim himself a god. Therefore Balaam's voice was given the power to inform the Gentiles: do not go astray after this man, "God is not a man" [a man can never be God]; and if he says that he is God—he is lying. That is the meaning of the verse, "God is not a man that He should lie."

Later, Balaam made another statement, whose *peshat* is not at all clear to us, and has been variously translated as: "He pronounced his oracle: 'O who will live (or: survive) when God does this (or: the setting of [or by] God)' (*Bamidbar* 24:23)." On this, the Midrash too has something to say: "Woe! Who will live of that nation, that listens to the words of the man who makes himself God?" In this case, there is no doubt that this is a reference to Jesus. And again Balaam is depicted as a prophet, a true prophet, who warned the Gentiles of the world not to make that error. But he failed.

But in other cases we see, in statements by the Sages as well, a type of association between Balaam and Jesus—an association which is not meant to place Balaam in a positive light, but rather to condemn him. And this association goes so far that in some instances it appears—and not only does it appear, but it is impossible not to recognize the fact—that the use of the name Balaam is merely meant to be a euphemism for Jesus. There is a legendary story of the proselyte Onkelos—a well-known figure, who, according to what we are told of him, was a Roman of the upper class, who became acquainted with the Jewish religion, began to think of converting, and ultimately did so. But while he was deliberating about conversion, he raised up three people from the dead, by means of witchcraft, in order consult with them before taking this step. The three people he raised up were Titus, the destroyer of the Temple; Balaam; and Jesus. The first two, the non-Jews, spoke against Israel, and warned Onkelos not to join the Jewish people. Jesus praised the Jewish people, and advised him to join them. The Midrash then concludes: "Note what the difference is between Jewish sinners [this is a reference to Jesus] and the prophets of the Gentiles"—Balaam, the prophet to the Gentiles, condemns Israel and even agitates against it. Yet this Jew, even though he is an apostate, still feels close to the Jewish people.

One can add numerous such examples, and I will bring one more such Aggada, this a very astounding one. We are told that a certain *min* (a *min* was a member of one of the early Christian sects) asked one of the Sages of Israel: "Do you know, or have you learned or read or heard, how old Balaam was when he died?" (Here the reference is to the same Balaam who was killed by Israel under the leadership of Pinchas.) The Sage answered him: "We have no tradition about this, but as it states, 'Bloodthirsty and treacherous men will not live out half their days' (*Tehillim* 55:24), I assume that he did not reach the age of 35, that being half the life of man." The *min* then answered him, "You were right, because I found written in Balaam's notebook that he was 33 years old when Pinchas *lista'a* (the robber or murderer) killed him."

What is Balaam's notebook? In the Torah, we have no reference to Balaam having written any book, but the allusion to an age of 33 is very clear. That is a reference to the Christian tradition that Jesus died at the age of 33. And what then is Pinchas *lista'a*? This is a very strange expression. Of course, one can explain it literally: after Pinchas killed him, he was called by this name. But one of the modern Jewish scholars of the 19th century, who studied Jewish sources and Jewish history, brought a very keen interpretation, which is totally convincing: "Pinchas *lista'a*" is a corruption—deliberate or otherwise—of Pontius Pilate. Then everything is perfectly clear: in the notebook of Balaam, in other words, in the Gospels, it is stated that Jesus was 33 years old when he was killed by Pontius Pilate.

PINCHAS

The beginning of the *sidra* of *Pinchas* is a direct continuation of the end of the previous *sidra, Balak*: the affair of the daughters of Moab, with whom the Israelites whored, and the worship of Pe'or: the scandal which climaxed in the odious act of Zimri, who blasphemed the God of Israel and scorned His prophet, Moses, by having sexual relations in public. It was Pinchas who was zealous for God, for God's honor which had been desecrated, and who took the law into his own hands. In other words, he wanted to carry out God's judgment by himself carrying out the punishment for the blasphemer. Here, at the beginning of our *sidra*, we are told that because of this, Pinchas and his descendants have been granted a covenant of peace with God. The radical zealot, who in his zealotry for God sheds human blood, is the very same person who is granted God's covenant of peace. From this we can deduce that a person is not permitted to be zealous for God and carry out extreme measures such as these unless he is someone who deserves to be a man of peace— *shalom*—who is faithful—*shalem*—to God and man. Only if he is faithful to God and man is he permitted to carry out judgments against a sinner.

Now this *sidra* of *Pinchas* has a very close parallel, one which is well-known, which is part of the consciousness of all generations, in the figure of the zealous prophet who arose about 500 or 600 years after Pinchas—the prophet Elijah. He too is zealous for God, and it is because of this that he kills the prophets of the Ba'al and the Ashera. The parallel between these two events and these two people is so strong, that not only was the *parasha* of Elijah adopted as the *haftara* for the *sidra* of *Pinchas*, but in the aggadic tradition, the two characters are fused into one, and Elijah is none other than Pinchas, who miraculously remained alive for 500 or 600 years. Now we have a thousands of years' old tradition that the prophet Elijah is the harbinger of peace, and the concluding verse in the Prophets is a verse on the prophet Elijah, who will come back and reconcile fathers with sons and sons with fathers—and will bring peace between the generations. There is also a remarkable discussion in the Mishna which deals with the question of the function that Elijah will fulfill in the end of days, and it too concludes by stating that Elijah will come to bring about peace in the world. Again we have the same contradiction: the zealot, who out of his zeal for God even sheds blood, is none other than the harbinger of peace.

The zeal of a mortal for the God of Hosts, which brings him to commit the most severe of actions, is a problematic topic both ethically and religiously. Who is permitted to be a zealot for God? Who is permitted to take upon himself the right to act in accordance with this zeal? An Aggada presents this question very forcefully in regard to the deeds of Elijah.

Elijah kills the prophets of Ba'al and must flee the wrath of Isabel. He flees to the desert and is privileged to have God appear to him. God does not appear in fire or thunder, but in a still, small voice, and asks him: Elijah, what are you doing here? Elijah answers: I have fled from Israel, for, "I have been very zealous for the Lord God of Hosts: for the children of Israel have forsaken Your covenant, thrown down Your altars, and slain Your prophets with the sword" (I *Melakhim* 19:10), and I had to flee for my life. In this, he wishes to justify the actions which he took: "I have been very zealous for the Lord God of Hosts."

Elijah is given an answer by God for every detail which he mentioned. On his comment that, "the children of Israel have forsaken Your covenant," God says to him, Whose covenant did they forsake? Was it your covenant or Mine? After all, it was not your covenant, and who gave you the right to be zealous against those who forsook My covenant? As to "they have torn down Your altars," God says to him: Did they tear down your altars or Mine? In other words: Let Me take care of My honor which is desecrated, and don't assume for yourself the authority to be zealous on My behalf. And the words of God continue in an almost brutal fashion. When Elijah says, "they have slain Your prophets with the sword," God answers him: you are still alive, you are a prophet and you are alive—thus you cannot say that they have killed all the prophets of God.

Elijah is then disqualified from being a prophet to Israel. God tells him: Israel cannot withstand your zealotry. You were zealous at Shittim (this is a clear reference to Pinchas, who, according to the Aggada, is Elijah), and now you were zealous at Mount Carmel. You spilled blood there and you spilled blood here, in your zeal for the God of Hosts. That is a noble deed, but Israel cannot survive such zeal. Therefore Elijah must find another person to be a prophet over Israel, and that is Elisha.

This has significance for all times. In every generation and at every time, but especially in our time, there are people who speak in the name of faith in God, and assume for themselves the authority to be zealous on God's behalf. And the question is asked: Is their personality such, and are their qualities and their human and ethical level such, that they are worthy of being men of the covenant of peace—except that their zeal for God has forced them to carry out these severe actions? Whoever has these qualities, who by his nature and essence is a man of peace, who wishes to bring peace to the world—only that person is permitted, in extreme cases, to be zealous on behalf of God. And if he is not a person who deserves to have a covenant of peace, he has no right to be zealous on God's behalf. If he is zealous on behalf of God without being suited for doing so, he is nothing but a murderer.

MATOT-MASEI

The *sidrot* of *Matot* and *Masei*, which are read together this year (in most years they are read on separate *Shabbatot*) are always read in the midst of the Three Weeks, between the beginning of the period of remembrance of the destruction of Jerusalem, on the 17th of *Tammuz*, and the end of that period, on the 9th of *Av*. The content of these two *sidrot* has no connection to the destruction and the exile, which are the themes of these three weeks. But these two *sidrot*, and the one following them, *Devarim*—the *sidra* of *Shabbat Chazon*, which always precedes the 9th of *Av*—all have *haftarot* which contain powerful admonitions of the Jewish people and prophecies of the destruction.

The *haftara* of *Masei* is taken from Jeremiah 2—and Jeremiah was the prophet of the destruction. If we look at the topics involved, it appears that there is no connection between the content of the *sidra* and that of the prophecy on the destruction by Jeremiah, who lived 700 or 800 years after the Torah was given and after the *sidra* of *Masei*. But beyond the aim of having a *haftara* during the Three Weeks which contains admonition of the Jewish people for their sins and a prophecy of the destruction of the Land of Israel, there is also a remarkable verbal association between one of the verses in the *sidra* of *Masei* and a central verse in Jeremiah's rebuke.

Among the many things mentioned in the *sidra* is a stringent warning against bloodshed. And in the warning against shedding blood, which comes after the verse that states that blood which is spilled defiles the land, it states, "Do not, therefore, defile the land which you will inhabit, wherein I dwell: for I God dwell among the

Israelites" (*Bamidbar* 35:34). God does not dwell in the land, but among the Israelites. It is that fact which makes the land significant when the Jews dwell on it. God dwells among the people of Israel only if they make Him dwell among them. He does not dwell among them automatically. Therefore the verse warns us: "Do not, therefore, defile the land which you will inhabit." Had God dwelled in the land because of the sanctity of the land, how could the land have been defiled by anyone? But here we are told that it is possible to defile the land.

And about 800 years after Moses, the prophet Jeremiah prophesied. He did not prophesy about what should be done and what should not be done, but about what the conditions were like and what was being done. And Jeremiah said, "You entered and defiled My land, and made My heritage an abomination" (*Yirmiyahu* 2:7). Moses said, "Do not, therefore, defile the land which you will inhabit" (*Bamidbar* 35:34), while Jeremiah, 800 years later, said: "You entered and defiled My land." The same land which is known as God's land ("My land") and God's inheritance, has no immanent uniqueness, and man's action can defile God's land and make His inheritance an abomination.

Jeremiah did not speak only to his own generation. Most of the sayings of the prophets contain eternal messages. There were some prophecies which were said for their own time, and were directed at their time, but the greatest, most important and demanding statements of the prophets of Israel were words of truth and justice for all generations and all times.

And that verse in Jeremiah is directed at us as well. On the one hand, we are aware, or at least there are some among us who are aware, that we have returned and are rebuilding our home in this land as God's land and His inheritance, while on the other hand, this does not prevent us from endorsing and declaring holy that which both the Torah in the *sidra* of *Masei* and the prophet Jeremiah regard as acts of defilement and abomination.

There is nothing more dangerous than cloaking defilement in the garb of holiness. The land itself does not have any inherent quality which sanctifies everything done in it, but only that which is done in it has the potential of imparting holiness to the land. In a famous Mishna, which was stated hundreds of years later, we are told that "the Land of Israel is more hallowed than the other lands." On this, the Mishna asks: "What is its holiness? That one brings from it the *omer* and the *bikkurim* (the first fruits) and the showbread." In other words: it is the observance of the *mitzvot* relating to the land which imparts holiness to the land; it is not holy in itself. The Mishna does not state that the Land of Israel is holier than the other lands, but it is holier than the other lands in that *mitzvot* are observed in it that can only be observed in the Land of Israel, such as the three *mitzvot* mentioned in the Mishna. And if we do not observe these laws, but do the opposite of what the Torah demands of us, the land can be defiled and God's inheritance can become an abomination.

These words apply to us. We should think of what we do in the land, the land which is meant to be God's land and His inheritance.

CHUMASH

DEVARIM

DEVARIM

The *Shabbat* on which the *sidra* of *Devarim* is read is known as *Shabbat Chazon*, the *Shabbat* before the 9th of *Av*. It is known as this because the *haftara* that is read begins with the word *"chazon"* ("the vision" of Isaiah)—one of the most severe and harsh admonitions that was ever directed toward Israel in terms of what its obligations are, and of how its failure to fulfill its obligations would bring about the destruction.

At first glance, it would appear that there is no connection between this severe *haftara* and the *sidra* itself, which has nothing to do with destruction, but, on the contrary, deals with construction: the summary that Moses gives of the march of Israel through the desert on the way to the Promised Land. He enumerates all the times that the generation of the desert faltered; but in spite of all of these failures the nation has now arrived at the threshold of Cana'an, having crossed the border into it, and has begun occupying it. The people have already conquered the lands of Sichon and Og and converted their lands into their own territory. It is now certain that they will inherit all of the land and will acquire it from its earlier inhabitants, and the land will become Israel's inheritance.

All of these things appear to be independent of the nature and behavior and deeds of Israel, which will be granted the land, and will replace its prior inhabitants. This would seem to be something special in history. And this is said very clearly: "I have set the land before you: go in and occupy the land which God swore to your fathers, Abraham, Isaac, and Jacob, to give to them and to their descendants after them" (*Devarim* 1:8); and, "Your children...they will enter it, and to them I will give it, and they will inherit it" (1:39); and, "I have begun to give Sichon and his land into your hands: begin to possess it" (2:31); and, "So the Lord our God also delivered into our hands Og the king of Bashan, and all his people and his land...and we annihilated them" (3:3); and, "This land, we possessed it" (3:12); "The Lord your God has given you this land to possess it" (3:18).

But note: among all of these verses, which imply that Israel is unique in terms of what God chooses for it in history, there are also references to other nations, all the neighbors of Israel and their lands, including some that are historic enemies of Israel. And this is most astounding, for it would appear that these references have no direct connection to the conquest of Cana'an by Israel. Yet we are told about the Edomites, "Do not provoke them; for I will not give you of their land, not as much as a foot's breadth; because I have given Mount Seir to Esau in possession" (*Devarim* 2:5). The same term of possession is thus used in regard to another nation, which is no less than an enemy of Israel. And a few verses later we read, "Do not harass the Moabites, nor provoke them to battle: for I will not give you of their land as a possession; because I have given Ar to the descendants of Lot as a possession" (*Devarim* 2:9).

And just as with Israel and the Canaanites, we are told that the land which is now Moab was once inhabited by the Emites, whom the Moabites destroyed. And the text returns to the Edomites, "The Horites also dwelt once in Seir; but the descendants of Esau succeeded them, when they had destroyed them, and dwelled there instead of them" (*Devarim* 2:12). And here we are told clearly, "as Israel did to the land of his possession, which God gave to them." In other words, the history of the descendants of Esau is not different from that of the Israelites. The Israelites are not unique in their history. And again, a few verses later, Moses again refers back to the Ammonites and the Moabites, who live in the lands once occupied by the Refaites and the Zamzumites, "God destroyed them before them; and they succeeded them, and dwelled there instead of them.

As he did to the descendants of Esau, which dwelt in Seir, when He destroyed the Horites from before them; and they succeeded them, and dwelled there instead of them to this day" (*Devarim* 2:21–22)— identical language to that used in regard to what God did for Israel. Moreover, we are given a note about a nation which, it would appear, has no connection with the history of Israel, "The Avites who dwelled in Hazerim, near Azzah, the Caphtorites, who came from Caphtor, destroyed them, and dwelled there instead of them" (*Devarim* 2:23).

What is the meaning of these reports on the history of other nations, of those that conquered other lands and of one nation displacing another? This is to indicate that Israel's uniqueness does not consist of historical events. All of human history—the history of Israel and the history of the other nations—is either a matter of history taking its course or else one of Divine direction. And if Israel is special, it is not because of its having conquered the land, or having inherited it or having taken the place of other nations, but because of the duties imposed upon it in this land: in the obligations which it was given and which were not given to other nations, for whom, too, God displaced other nations, so that they might inherit their lands. There is, therefore, profound significance in the fact that this passage is read on *Shabbat Chazon*, before the 9th of *Av*.

Now we will discuss a term which forms a connection between the text of Lamentations, which refers to the 9th of *Av* (and Lamentations was written about a thousand years after the Torah), and the text of the *sidra* itself. In the narrative of Israel's coming to the land, or its journey on its way to the land, Moses complains of his failure with Israel on that journey, "How (in Hebrew, *eikha*) can I myself alone bear your trouble, and your burden, and your strife?" (*Devarim* 1:12). And 800 years later, the prophet Isaiah comments on the failure in the conquest of the land and Israel's occupation of it, for it did not fulfill its obligations, "How (*eikha*) has the faithful city become a whore! It was endowed with justice; righteousness lodged in it; but now murderers" (*Yeshaya* 1:21). (These words sound as if they are addressed to us today; and 150 years after Isaiah came the destruction.) And in the great lamentation, which tradition, possibly aggadic, attributes to Jeremiah himself (and if it was not by him, it was by someone of his generation), we are told, "How (*eikha*) does the city sit solitary" (*Eikha* 1:1).

On their way to conquer the land: "How (*eikha*) can I myself alone bear your trouble, and your burden, and your strife?" When they dwelled in the land again: "How (*eikha*) has the faithful city become a whore." And in the end, again: "How (*eikha*) does the city sit solitary?"

This is historiosophy of profound significance, and the use of the term, *eikha*, both in the *sidra* on coming to the land, and the 9th of *Av*, which commemorates the destruction and the exile, is not coincidental. It is not a matter of the calendar working out that way, but an indication of the significance and the meaning of the course of history of Israel, and to a certain extent, to the historical relations and ties between the events in the histories of all nations.

VA'ETCHANAN

Va'etchanan is the *sidra* of *Shabbat Nachamu*, the *Shabbat* after the 9th of *Av*, and that is why the *haftara* chosen for this *Shabbat* is the great chapter of consolation in the book of Isaiah. But this is not at all simple, for it is just the *sidra* of *Va'etchanan*, which is followed by the message of consolation, which contains the short Torah reading for the 9th of *Av* itself, that being the *parasha* of the destruction, "When you will beget children, and grandchildren, and will have dwelled long in the land...." (*Devarim* 4:25, 26) (this is stated even before the major part of the land was conquered, and tells us what will happen, or is liable to happen: the Israelites will corrupt the land and become corrupt themselves). Moses warns Israel, "You will soon vanish from the land...you will not live long in it, but will perish" (*Devarim* 4:26). It is just on *Shabbat Nachamu* that the Torah reading includes the *parasha* which, because of its content, is read on the 9th of *Av*. It is true that immediately after this warning, "You will perish," hope is offered for the future, "You will turn back to the Lord your God ...and He will not forget the sworn covenant with your fathers" (*Devarim* 4:30, 31). God does not forget. The basic question is whether *you* will remember or forget.

And in that small *parasha* we also find, "You had been shown, that you might know, that the Lord is God; there is none else beside Him.... Know therefore this day, and consider it in your heart, that the Lord is God in heaven above, and on earth below: there is none else" (*Devarim* 4:35, 39). You had been shown, but that is no guarantee that you see. God showed it to you, but you did not see— and that is why your future is not secure.

What is interesting is that in the *haftara* (which, it would appear, is a message of consolation, beginning with the lofty words that are so well-known by many, "'Comfort, comfort My people,' says your God. 'Comfort Jerusalem, and tell it, its time of desolation has come to an end, and its iniquity has been pardoned: for it has received of God's hand double for all its sins'"—*Yeshaya* 40:1, 2), is, if one delves into it closely, after the great call of consolation for the destruction, a strong admonition against the people who refrain to recognize God's deeds. Even though they have been shown so that they should know that He is God, they do not see this. Thus we see that the matters of the admonition and destruction on the one hand, and of consolation and return on the other, are bound together, and cannot be separated.

The *sidra* of *Va'etchanan* includes two of the most central *parshiyot* in the Torah: the Ten Commandments, which are repeated in *Va'etchanan* with some stylistic changes as compared to the Ten Commandments in the *sidra* of *Yitro*; and the second *parasha*, which has become the first paragraph of the *Shema*, the prime document of faith in Israel. I will discuss the *Shema* next week, for next week's *parasha* includes the second paragraph of the *Shema*, *Vehaya im shamo'a*, and I will discuss the connection between the two *parshiyot*.

But here I would like to discuss the beginning of the *sidra* of *Va'etchanan*, which, it would appear, has nothing to do with these matters and is, in a certain sense, a personal concern of Moses, in which he pleads to God to annul the decree that he will not enter the Land of Israel. A few weeks ago, I discussed the fact that Moses is not aware of the fact that he has sinned, but regards the decree against him as not being justified. When he pleads to God here, he does not ask for forgiveness of his sin, but for the annulment of the decree. And this is depicted in a most dramatic form in many *midrashim*, which deal with the great debate between Moses and God regarding God's decree against him, and his demand that the decree—one which he regards as an injustice toward himself—be annulled, and God's refusal to accede to him. Here, I will only discuss one of these *midrashim*, because it has a message which affects us.

At the end of a major discussion between God and Moses, when Moses demands that God prolong his life so that he will be able to enter the land, God says to him: "You are demanding life. And you yourself—did I tell you to kill the Egyptian?" God suddenly reminds Moses of something that had happened forty years earlier: he killed a human being. It is true that he killed an Egyptian who was beating an Israelite—but he killed a person, and if that is so—how can he demand life? The dispute takes a most dramatic turn, when Moses has the audacity to respond to God: "You are punishing me for killing an Egyptian—but you killed the Egyptian firstborn who had not sinned. Should I then die for a single Egyptian?" To this, God has a decisive answer: "Are you comparing yourself to Me? It is I who give life and take it away—whatever life a person has comes from Me, and I have the right to take it back. But you, are you able to give life? Who gave you the right to take life?"

It is fitting that we should think of these words that one of the *Amora'im* stated in this Aggada. Even in such a case, where Moses killed an Egyptian who was striking an Israelite, where his action was justified, we are confronted by a disturbing problem: May a person kill another, for whatever reason and whatever the justification? One must therefore think of those situations where we regard it as legitimate to sacrifice human life, or to take human life, for something which appears to be more precious than human life. And yet the question remains: Are we assuming for ourselves the authority which only God has? For it is He who gives life and only He who has the right to take it.

EKEV

One of the *parshiyot* of the *sidra* of *Ekev*, a *sidra* with many topics, is the *parasha* of *"Vehaya im shamo'a"*—"if you will listen" (*Devarim* 1:13–21), the second paragraph of the *Shema*, the first being in the previous *sidra* of *Va'etchanan*. It is these two *parshiyot* which are written on the parchment scroll which forms the *mezuza* on the doors of those Jews who observe the Torah and its *mitzvot*, and it is these two, together with the *parasha* of *tzitzit*—about which I was privileged to speak a few weeks ago—that form the entire *Shema*: the first *mitzva* in the oral Torah, which sets out one's life's program in accordance with the Torah and *mitzvot*—and that oral Torah begins with "From what time may the *Shema* be said at night?"

One should say a few words about the connection between the first two of these *parshiyot*, which together are the great document of faith of Judaism. There is a major difference between the two. Not only are they two different worlds, but they are two contrary worlds, but yet they come from the same source and are placed next to one another in the *Shema*.

When I speak of the first *parasha*, I do not necessarily refer to the first verse, which, among Jews, is our great motto or the declaration of our faith ("Hear O Israel, God is our God, God is One"), but the second verse, which contains, in some sense, the operative word of behavior in accordance with faith: "You will love the Lord your God with all your heart and with all your soul and with all your might" (*Devarim* 6:5), the love of God as an absolute demand upon man. The implication of an absolute demand is that it is not presented as something which stems from certain facts from which it is derived, but is presented in terms of itself. No reason is given for the *mitzva* to love God, nor is it strengthened by what one would today refer to as sanctions. It does not say: "if you observe the following, it will be good for you, and if, heaven forbid, you do not observe it—you will be punished." This *mitzva* is valid in and of itself. In philosophical parlance, such a *mitzva* is referred to as categorical. And regarding the profound significance of the *mitzva*, "You will love the Lord your God," which gives no reasons and is not linked to any promise, it is on this great verse in the written Torah that the greatest figure in the world of the oral Torah, R. Akiva, made his well-known comment: "'with all your soul'—even if He takes away your soul" (i.e., your life).

The exact opposite of the connotation of the first paragraph of the *Shema* is the second paragraph, *Vehaya*, in which explanations and arguments are given for the *mitzva* to love God and to serve Him. This paragraph, too, mentions the love of God ("to love the Lord your God with all your hearts and with all your souls"—*Devarim* 11:13), but here we are given a reason for this love, and the observance of the *mitzva* is strengthened by sanctions. The very word "if" at the beginning of the *parasha* ("*if* you will listen"), and the word "lest" later on ("*lest* your heart be deceived") indicate that an alternative exists of violating this *mitzva*, with everything which will follow as a result. In regard to the categorical *mitzva*, the problem of violation of the *mitzva* is not raised at all, whereas in the second *parasha*, the acceptance of the Yoke of Heaven and the Yoke of Torah and *mitzvot* appears to be presented in a utilitarian manner: "If you listen…I will give rain in your fields…take care, lest your heart be deceived…and God will become angry with you, and He will close the heavens and there will be no rain…and you will soon perish from the good land…."(*Devarim* 11:13–17).

If the first *parasha* presents the faith of R. Akiva, who died to sanctify God's name, the second paragraph would appear to present the view of a man who had once been R. Akiva's colleague, but who had later become known as *Acher*—Elisha ben Avuya. And a story, which may possibly not be historical but nevertheless has a deep meaning, explains how it was that a *Tanna*, one who was a great Torah scholar, Elisha ben Avuya, became *Acher*—"the other one"— whose name is not mentioned anymore. We are told that once Elisha ben Avuya was walking past an orchard or a vineyard, where the owner of the field told his son to climb a tree to a certain bird's nest, where he was to send away the mother bird and take the eggs. The child did as commanded by his father, or, in other words, fulfilled two *mitzvot*: honoring one's father and sending away the mother bird—about both of which the Torah states, "that your days may be prolonged." Yet the child fell from the tree and died.

Elisha ben Avuya then exclaimed: "where is the long life of this one?"—and he became *Acher*.

One may say that, unlike R. Akiva, who explains "with all your soul" to refer to even when He takes your life, Elisha ben Avuya understood faith in terms of the way it seems to appear in the second paragraph of the *Shema*: if you listen, it will be good for you. Yet here he saw that this was not so.

How are we to understand the juxtaposition of the two passages and their inclusion in the great *mitzva* of the *Shema*? This relates to the two great concepts which exist in Jewish faith, both of which are legitimate: *lishma*—"for its own sake," and *shelo lishma*—"not for its own sake." Both are ways to serve God, and the Torah recognizes both. In terms drawn from the philosophical world, one can say: faith and Torah whose significance is deontological, and faith and Torah whose significance is consequentialistic. The first *parasha* of the *Shema* is an expression of "Torah for its own sake," that being the love of God without instrumental significance, and its aim is contained within itself. Therefore no reason is given and there are no sanctions. Had one been able to give a reason for it, it would have lost its significance as a categorical command, as something a person accepts because he sees its value in itself. But not every person is capable of that. We know the saying of Maimonides, that the Torah permitted man to serve God and to observe the *mitzvot* with the hope of being rewarded, and to refrain from sin because of his fear of punishment. It is to these people that the second paragraph of the *Shema* is addressed. Even a believing Jew, who observes the Torah and *mitzvot* in the spirit of "*Vehaya im shamo'a*," of the second paragraph of the *Shema*, is an upright Jew. But the purpose of faith is not the results which stem from the fact that there is faith, but the faith itself. And that is what the first paragraph of the *Shema* expresses, and it was for this that R. Akiva gave his life.

The love of God, the fear of God, and the worship of God are all intermingled, and cannot be separated, and that is the summary of the content of the two *sidrot* of *Va'etchanan* and *Ekev*.

You will love the Lord → Your God....	And these words which I command you....
to fear the Lord your God →	to serve the Lord your God
and to love Him →	to observe the *mitzvot* of God and His statutes that I command you
You will fear the Lord → your God	Him you will serve
to love the Lord your God →	And to serve Him with all your heart and all your soul

And you will observe the *mitzvot*   ← and to fear Him
of the Lord your God

So too do we see this in the *sidra* of *Re'eh*, which is the topic of our
next talk:

To love the Lord your God →   You will observe His charge and
      His statutes and His judgments
      and His *mitzvot*

And this is the way Maimonides summarized the matter, about
2,500 years after it was stated in the Torah: "...for all that the Torah
intends is directed toward a single purpose—and that is to worship
the Exalted and Revered Name. And this purpose is achieved by the
practice of the *mitzvot*."

RE'EH

In the Torah, we are accustomed to appeals to the Israelites in the form of "listen." Our *sidra* begins with the injunction, "see," and what we are to heed refers to a matter of the highest importance: man's deciding between good and bad, a decision phrased here as distinguishing between a blessing and a curse. But the idea of choosing is repeated, in a more succinct and profound form, in the same book of Deuteronomy, in the *sidra* of *Nitzavim*, and I hope that I will be able to deal with this great topic at the appropriate time.

After this great appeal, our *sidra* begins as a kind of law code. This, indeed, is the major part of Deuteronomy—a review of the *mitzvot*, with additions and amplifications on what was said at Sinai. The *sidra* of *Re'eh* deals almost entirely with the *mitzvot* related to public matters. These matters do, of course, refer to every individual too, but they deal primarily with the organization of the community within a judicial and political framework in accordance with the Torah.

The first *mitzva* is the great and important one of eliminating idolatry from the Land of Israel; the idolatry of the Canaanites and the manifestations of idolatry in Israel—the false prophet, the one who entices others to idolatry, and the idolatrous city. And, as opposed to this, we have the designation of, "the place that God will choose" (*Devarim* 12:5), in which, and only in which, the worship of God is to be carried out by sacrifices (unlike any other place, where the worship of God is embodied in the observance of the *mitzvot*, without any sacrifices). The setting aside of this place for the sacrificial ritual is a very important matter, and numerous studies and discussions about the history of the biblical period deal with it. This is neither the time nor the proper framework to discuss this, and we will content ourselves by noting that Jerusalem is not mentioned here as the place that God will choose; one may possibly conclude from this—unlike the prevalent view in biblical criticism—that this was stated in the time before Jerusalem had become the chosen site, or, in other words, before the time of the monarchy.

Determining the place that God will choose relates to three *mitzvot* in our *sidra*: the second tithe (an arrangement for making the pilgrimage to the chosen place economically possible); the paschal sacrifice, not as a family matter but as worship in the Temple; and the three pilgrimage festivals.

Another topic, whose importance is also communal, social and even political, is the great social legislation of the Torah, which is expressed in three important institutions: the tithe for the poor, the cancellation of debts in the *shemitta* year, and the general law of giving charity.

In the little time available to us, I would like to discuss, and this too only cursorily, the issue of social legislation, within which two very famous verses appear, and one should examine the relationship and connection—or possibly the contradiction—between them. In regard to the cancellation of debts, we are told, "There will be no poor among you, for God will greatly bless you...."(*Devarim* 15:4). Then, in regard to the giving of charity, in regard to not closing one's hand and hardening one's heart, it states, "The poor will never vanish from the land" (*Devarim* 15:11). The contradiction between these two verses is only illusory. One should not understand "there will be no poor" as a promise, but as a demand made on us. We have the duty to prevent circumstances whereby there will be poor among us, by observing the *mitzvot* of cancelling debts in the *shemitta* year and observing all the other *mitzvot* with social significance. Without these provisions, which we are obligated to enforce, the other verse will be true: "the poor will never vanish from the land." Poverty does not vanish of itself. In other words, in a social system in which there is poverty, the poverty will not disappear of itself, and one should not trust to it disappearing through the One who "opens His hand and satisfies the needs of every living creature" (*Tehillim* 145:16). Rather, God demands that we are to see to it that there will be no poor within the land.

This matter is important, because it is from it we can understand many things both in the Torah and in the Prophets, which seem to imply that certain promises will be fulfilled regardless. But the connotation of a Divine promise is not like a pagan oracle, which tells us what will occur in the future. Had that been the case, that would not have religious significance. A Divine promise is always a demand made of man: this is the way things ought to be. This is the way that *Tosafot*, a major work of rabbinic Judaism, about 2,500 years after the giving of the Torah, understands prophetic promises, and this has extremely profound significance specifically in the realm of faith: "No prophet predicts but that which should be"—and there is no guarantee that that is the way it will be. This applies equally to Israel's redemption and its return to its land: all of this is what *should be*, but whether it will be that way depends, at least to some extent, on us.

The topic with which we are dealing is a type of paradigm of this: it is fitting that there should be no poor, but that is not guaranteed, even though the Torah says "there will be no poor, for God will bless you." God's blessing is conditional on the fact that we will do everything that we are obligated to in order to get rid of poverty, and if that is not done, then—"the poor will never vanish from the land." And from this we should learn something about the great destination and the great promises to the entire Jewish people: we may note that remarkable promises, among the most remarkable of all, were given by Amos and Jeremiah and Ezekiel to the ten tribes, in that they would return from their exile. These prophecies were not fulfilled, but that does not undermine our faith in "the prophets of truth and righteousness." What they prophesied was what should be, and we were evidently not fit to have these promises fulfilled.

SHOFTIM

The *sidra* of *Shoftim* is the direct continuation of the *sidra* of *Re'eh*, and contains a group of *mitzvot* which deal primarily with organizing the community in accordance with the Torah within a framework of judiciary, administration and statehood. The *sidra* refers primarily to judges and court officers—the judicial power, which also has legislative authority (here there is no separation of the legislative and the judicial powers), and also includes instructions regarding judicial procedure and the laws of testimony. Afterwards we have the major question of the executive power—is it to be linked to the institution of the monarchy? "The *parasha* of the king" is discussed in the oral Torah from different points of view and in different directions, even contradicting one another.

The *sidra* then reverts to the *mitzva* of exterminating idolatry and whatever follows in its wake, and this includes some practices which persist to this very day: witchcraft and conjuring up the dead, and all the other superstitions which appear, sometimes even today, in a seemingly religious garb, but which, in reality, are nothing but the abomination of idolatry in a different guise. Then there are the laws of warfare—a *parasha* of tremendous significance, but we are unable to deal with it within our framework. The *sidra* stresses forcefully the prohibition against shedding blood (following on from the laws of war): the laws governing murder, and the special provisions for inadvertent killing and the establishment of the cities of refuge; and, in this context, mentions the *eglah arufah*—the rite of the slaughter of the heifer which is killed when a person is found murdered. And it is in regard to the *eglah arufah*—evidently a specific detail concerning murder at the end of the *sidra*—that I would like to pause.

A murder was committed, and, to use modern-day parlance, it was not "solved," or, in the language of the Torah, "If the body of a slain person is found on the soil which the Lord your God gives you to possess it, lying in the field, and it is not known who has slain him" (*Devarim* 21:1). Among Israel, on the Land of Israel, a person was killed. The blame is on the entire community in whose midst the murder occurred, and a special rite is held in order to make the people realize the enormity of the fact that such a thing happened among them. The elders of the city "which is next to the slain man" must meet and perform the rite known as *eglah arufah*, and must state aloud, "Our hands have not shed this blood, neither have our eyes seen it" (*Devarim* 21:7)—and yet we are guilty, and therefore—"Be merciful, O Lord, to your people Israel, whom You have redeemed...." (*Devarim* 21:8). But in the Mishna, in a text written possibly 1,500 years after the Torah, we read: "When the number of murderers increased, the rite of *eglah arufah* lapsed." This religious rite is meaningful in a society in which murder is something which is abhorrent and an exceptional occurrence. In a society which is corrupt and where murder is a common occurrence, there is no reason to pretend that we are shocked by an unsolved murder. In such a society, there is a certain measure of hypocrisy in such a rite. The society must be purged of the daily occurrences of murder, and only then, when murder is an abnormal occurrence, is there reason to hold the ceremony.

We find an analogous situation in regard to sexual crime. The Torah established a severe trial for a woman suspected of having committed adultery, where she is tested through having to drink the bitter waters. This is the only case in the entire Torah where a person is put on trial, not before a human court, but, as it were, before the heavenly court. Now, this type of test can only be of significance in a society where chastity is the norm, and a case of suspected adultery arouses revulsion. Therefore, in the Mishna which I mentioned, it also states: "When adultery became common, the rite of the bitter waters was abolished." If a society is saturated with sexual immorality and licentiousness, there is no reason to be shocked at the case of a suspected adulteress; one ought instead to try to reform the society. Only in an upright society, where murder is exceptional, must one react with the *eglah arufah* in the case of an unsolved murder. In a society where sexual probity is the norm, one should react with the use of the bitter waters in a case of suspected adultery. But if the society is corrupt—there is no reason for these ceremonies.

From this, we can learn much for our own situation. There are certain halakhic demands that are worth presenting (and, of course, an effort should be made to obtain them) only within a society which—as a body—accepts the validity of the *halakha*. If it generally does not recognize it, then demands for certain details of *halakha* to be observed become absurd. In a society in which there are many murderers, there is no reason to have an *eglah arufah* ceremony, and in a society in which adultery is widespread, there is no reason to have the bitter waters. In a society and a state which are not based on the recognition of the obligation to observe the Torah, there is no reason to investigate whether some specific law of the state is in accordance with the *halakha*. By directing our thoughts and actions to just these details, in order to have these observed in accordance with the *halakha*, and this within the framework of a society and state which are not in accordance with the Torah and *halakha*—we make the struggle for the Torah and its *mitzvot* into a caricature.

In a society in which public life, as based on government and law, involves the operation of ports and airports on *Shabbat*, where hundreds of factories work on *Shabbat* with governmental permission, where there are government radio and television on *Shabbat*, where thousands of private vehicles drive on *Shabbat*, where there are soccer matches which attract tens of thousands of spectators on *Shabbat*, and all of this with the official religious representatives participating in this government (in the central government and in the administration of cities)—the struggle against the opening of another movie house on *Shabbat* makes religion into a mockery. In a society where large parts within it, of all social classes, both the educated and the ignorant, have ruled that "You will not commit adultery" and "there will not be a harlot" does not apply, and that such phenomena are even understandable—the requirement that marriage must be in accordance with *halakha* is only a desecration of the institute of religious marriage, a desecration of the Torah, and only serves to increase the number of *mamzerim* in Israel.

Mend the society, mend the state—and then you are permitted, and are even obliged, to be concerned that the details within the framework of the society and the state should be in accordance with the demands of the Torah. As long as you do not struggle for a change of the image of the Jewish people, you cannot struggle for certain details in the lifestyle of the members of this community, and certainly not for details in the laws of that state, that the community—which has not assumed for itself the Yoke of the Torah and *mitzvot*—is establishing for itself.

KI TEITZEI

Among the many *mitzvot* in the *sidra* of *Ki Teitzei*, we will attempt to touch on two. And I state clearly "to touch," because both of them have very far-reaching implications on extremely profound problems, that we can merely hint at.

The one appears to be simply a technical matter: the *mitzva* to build a *ma'akeh*—a parapet around one's roof, "When you build a new house, make a parapet for your roof, that you do not bring blood upon your house, if any faller falls from it" (*Devarim* 22:8). This is a *mitzva* which seems to be part of a building code, and its purpose is caution: preventing danger to human life. But this matter, which seems so obvious, presents major problems, specifically in the realms of faith and of ethics. Our Sages have already noted these problems, and dwelled on the second half of the verse, "if any faller falls from it." How can a person be referred to as a "faller" before he has fallen? Is the Torah telling us here that no person falls unless it was decreed in heaven that this should occur, and therefore he is considered to be a "faller" even before he falls? According to a very widely held view of the concept of personal providence, "a person does not raise a finger below (i.e., on earth) unless it is decreed so above" (i.e., in heaven). But if that is the case, we can ask the obvious question: If it was decreed that the person will fall and die, what purpose does the parapet serve? And if it was not decreed—why have a parapet? In accordance with this view, the Midrash states: "If any faller falls from it—this person is predestined (or: "deserves") to fall since the creation" of the world.

This is a formulation of what is referred to as the deterministic viewpoint: whatever will happen is a necessary result of what preceded it, and that which preceded it is also a necessary result of what preceded it, and similarly, we can trace everything back infinitely, or until we can fine a prime cause. What preceded everything? The creation of the world by God's will. According to this, it is God's will that the causes and effects follow in a progression, with each effect being the cause of what follows it, until we arrive at this person's falling from the roof. But if that is so, then there is no reason to build a parapet.

Here we are confronted by the problem which has occupied thinkers, both believers and philosophers, among Jews and among the Gentiles, from time immemorial: the constancy of the natural reality to which man belongs, and man's free choice. And one may say that it is just in the formulation of our Sages: "this person deserves to fall from the creation"—that we have a hint at a possible explanation. What was determined in the creation? The laws of nature, the causality of nature. And in terms of this causality, this person indeed deserved to fall if he is not careful, or if the person who builds the house does not bother to build a parapet for his house. Whether he will actually fall—that depends on man's behavior, and that is not a contradiction to Providence. Providence is expressed in the fact that the person would deserve to fall if there would be no parapet. This consideration—even though its validity is sharply disputed among philosophical and theological thinkers—is an opening for understanding many things in the *mitzva* system.

We link this immediately to another *mitzva*, a very strange one, which is also in *Ki Teitzei*, whose strangeness was already noted by our Sages, and one which we too must pause at: the *mitzva* of the rebellious son. The rebellious son does not obey his father and his mother, and that is why he is stoned. The oral Torah seems to give an explanation for this: that he is "sentenced because of his future" (i.e., what will eventually become of him). But this is illogical, and is in total contradiction to the conception of punishment—not only in the Torah, but in any orderly legal system: that a person is never punished for what he is liable to do in the future, as long as he has not done anything yet. The explanation given for the death penalty to the rebellious son is that "in the future, this person will be an armed robber": as now, in his youth, he is a glutton and drunkard, and does not obey his father and mother, he will eventually become an armed robber or a murderer. Yet, at this moment he is not an armed robber or a murderer, but is only a glutton and a drunkard. Where, then, do we find that a person is sentenced to death because we are afraid that he may turn out bad and may then be guilty of an offense carrying the death penalty?

The conclusion of the Talmud is very interesting: "The case of the rebellious son never happened and will never happen." The Torah tells us what is fitting to happen, in terms of what we may be permitted to call Divine justice. In terms of Divine justice, where to God the future is as apparent as the present, this person, who will eventually become a brigand or a murderer, deserves to die now and ought to be killed. But we do not have the right to implement his law.

And indeed, when the *halakha* discusses the law of the rebellious son, it adds so many restrictions as to make the implementation of the law an impossibility. I would like to note only one point, which appears anecdotal, but is of very profound significance. As the Torah states that the father and mother must bring their son to the court and say, "This our son is stubborn and rebellious, he will not obey our voice" (*Devarim* 21:20), and as "our voice" is stated in the singular (rather than "our voices"), the *halakha* rules that if the father and mother do not have the same-sounding voice, the law of the rebellious son does not apply in that instance.

Now, as we know, it is unrealistic to expect a man and a woman to have voices that sound the same, so we see that the law cannot be enforced, but can only remain as a threat. The person deserves to die, but we do not carry out any punishment.

We should also note that the distinction between what ought to be done, and what we are permitted to do, is very far-reaching. It is possible that this is the most profound explanation of the fact that the written Torah contains 36 sins or crimes for the violation of which the penalty is death, whereas in the oral Torah all of this is in practice annulled, as the death penalty can only be imposed provided that there are two witnesses that warn the person in advance not to carry out this action, inform him of the penalty should he disobey them, and then have the person respond that he intends to carry out the action regardless, and that makes the death penalty outside the realm of the realistic. The same is true for bodily injury. The Torah states: "as he has done, so will it be done to him...eye for eye, tooth for tooth...." (*Vayikra* 24:19–20), yet the *halakha* rules that the compensation is monetary: a person injuring another must pay for the damage, the pain, the medical costs, the person's incapacity, and humiliation. In terms of Divine justice, the people deserved to have done to them what they had done to their fellows, but we are not permitted to act in accordance with Divine justice. Thus, without undermining the written Torah, the oral Torah places so many restrictions about it, that it cannot be implemented as such.

I would like to remind you that a few weeks ago I had the opportunity to apply the notion of "ought" or "deserves to be" (or "should be") to another matter—prophecies about the future: "A prophet foretells but what ought to take place." The prophet presents a future which must be strived for, and which one must attempt to bring to fruition, without any guarantee that this will actually be realized. The term "deserves" (or "ought") refers to the *mitzvot*, to law and justice, and to forecasting the future. Every prophecy deserves to happen—and it depends on man whether those things which deserve to happen will or will not happen.

KI TAVO

In this imposing *sidra*, *Ki Tavo*, the *sidra* which contains the blessings and the curses, the marvelous destiny in the future, and the terrible *tokhecha*, or admonition, I would like to discuss only two verses. It is these two verses that I dare to regard as a type of key to understanding the most basic principle in the world of Jewish faith regarding the relationship between Israel and its God—or, if we wish to be very bold, between the God of Israel and His nation. As they cannot be read to you here in the original Hebrew, I will use one of the various English translations, the one I consider to be the most appropriate: "You have recognized God this day as your God, to walk in His ways and to keep His laws, His *mitzvot* and his judgments, and to obey Him. And God has recognized you this day as His chosen people, as He promised you, to keep all His *mitzvot*."

First of all, we must pause at the term (here translated as "recognize") which appears only one time in the Bible, in the two verses above, with the Hebrew root "AMR" in the *hiphil* conjugation. There are many interpretations of this word, in the traditional commentaries on the Torah as well as in the different ancient and modern translations. Most of the commentators and the translators— and it appears to me, that we too, if we read these verses without any preconceptions—understand that this word says something about the ties between God and the Jewish people. There are those who translate it in terms of choosing, or in the sense of acquiring (or appropriating something precious), and I have also heard, but cannot judge this, that in Arabic there is a word of the same root which indicates the ties between a bridegroom and his bride. It is clear that that sense would be most appropriate for these two verses.

Going back, it would seem to appear that the one is linked to the other: you recognized God today to be your God, and God recognized you to be His chosen people. Is there a causal tie between these two? Is it because we choose God to be our God that He chooses us as His chosen nation? Or could it even be the opposite: Is it because God chooses us as His chosen people that we chose Him as our God? Or are they parallel to one another, and there is no causal link between the two?

Now, if we again examine the two verses, we will see that the connection between them is far more profound than all our hypotheses: "You have chosen God this day to be your God"—and how is this choice realized? It is through the fact that you have obligated yourself to keep His *mitzvot*. That is the way we relate to God. And what about the second verse, "And God has chosen you this day to be His chosen people"? One might have thought that just as Israel's choice is expressed in the observance of the *mitzvot*, one would expect that God's choice of Israel should be expressed in something that God will do for Israel. But what does the Torah state here? God's choice of Israel is expressed in the same terms as Israel's choice of God—in the fact that Israel observes His *mitzvot*.

These two verses not only do not speak of matters which parallel one another, nor are they two items where one is the cause of the other, but they are one. The relationship between God and His nation, and the relationship between the nation and its God, are not two things juxtaposed one against the other, but are the very same thing. The fact that the people accept God as their God is the very fact that God chooses this people. That is the most profound meaning of the concept of the Jews as the chosen people.

This idea finds expression in one of the greatest documents, possibly the greatest and most exalted that exists in regard to faith in Judaism, in the prayer which (as I understand it) is the most momentous of all prayers, even though there is a tendency to underrate it, because it is said so frequently—the *Aleynu* prayer, which is the key passage of the prayer of *Rosh Hashana*: "We praise the Master of all, and ascribe greatness to the Creator." Why must we do so? Is it because of what He did for us? No—we do so because "we bend our knees and bow down and thank Him." We praise Him because we worship Him, because we have the privilege of worshipping Him.

It is in this that we are different from the other nations and "our portion is not that of the other nations": it is not because the Jew who observes the Torah and the *mitzvot* lives longer than a person who does not observe them, and not because we enjoy life more; nor because the Jewish people's fate, objectively, is superior to that of other people—but because the Jewish people serve God. That is why our hope for the future—"We therefore hope in You, O Lord our God...."—does not speak of the future of the individual Jew, nor of the future of the Jewish people, but of our hope that the entire world will acknowledge God, just as the Jewish people (at least the ideal Jewish people, not the actual one) acknowledges God. This is not a grant which we are given, but a great and difficult task which was imposed upon us—that God is our God in that we acknowledge Him as our God.

NITZAVIM-VAYELEKH

The short *sidra* of *Nitzavim* is one of the most remarkable in the Torah, if one can grade the different *sidrot*. It contains some of the most exalted and profound ideas that a person can understand in God's words as addressed to man. One of these is the short section, of ten verses, which is the *parasha* of *teshuva* (commonly translated as repentance), the only *parasha* in the Torah in which repentance is presented in all its profundity and acuteness. The word *teshuva* is derived from the Hebrew root "SHUV"—to return to something.

Now in this *parasha* of *teshuva* (*Devarim* 30:1–10), we find the following: Moses speaks about the future of some indefinite date, in which, in his words, there will be the fulfillment of, "You will take—*vehasheivota*—to heart" (what you have done and what befell you), and "you will return—*veshavta*—to the Lord your God" and "the Lord your God will bring back—*veshav*—your captives—*shevutekha*" (*Devarim* 30:1–10). In this passage, we find four related (or similar?) terms, three of them derived from the root "SHUV": you will take to your heart; you will return to the Lord your God; God will bring back your captives (the root of the word for captivity, *shevut*, is the Hebrew equivalent of "SHVH," but this is a play on words), and afterwards, at the end of the *parasha*, we find again, "You will return—*tashuv*—and obey the voice of God…God will again—*yashuv*—rejoice over you for good, as He rejoiced over your fathers…if you return—*tashuv*—to the Lord your God with all your heart, and with all your soul."

All of these concepts: taking to heart, returning, repenting, and redemption from captivity, are intertwined, and cannot be separated from one another. Analyzing the connection between them is not something we can do in the few minutes available to us. One can certainly say, and without exaggeration, that even in a life devoted to pondering the problems of faith, this subject could not be exhausted.

Another section in this *sidra*, of five verses (*Devarim* 30:15–19), deals with a different topic, and one can safely say that all of man's thinking—and in this case, not only that of the believer, but that of every person who thinks—is contained within it. Is man's free choice possible? From this *sidra*, it appears that it is indeed possible, for the *sidra* states: "See, I have set before you this day life and good, and death and evil"—this is offered to man. And four verses later we find, "I have set before you life and death, blessing and curse: therefore choose life."

The question that one may ask is to what extent man is free to choose, as part of natural reality, in which one thing by necessity follows from another. In philosophical terms, this is known as determinism. Man is unable to think of any event—and not only in the physical world, but even in man's psychic reality—which does not have a reason which compels its occurrence. From the time that human thought, both in Judaism and in foreign thinking, has dealt with the problem of man's knowledge of himself, it has struggled with this question. It is possible that it is a question which cannot be answered, because it always winds up with antinomies.

But one should pause at one topic. The naive ones among us, that claim that man's free will is one of the basic principles of religious faith, make a grave error. Empirically, as can be seen from beliefs and religions which have existed and which exist to this day, we are aware that some trends of a very deep religious faith, which regard man's existence from the perspective of his status before God, are also compatible with the belief that all of man's existence, including his will, his intentions and actions, is decreed from on High. This problem is a matter of dispute both among believers and among thinkers who are far from religious faith.

I will limit myself to no more than a hint. In the world of Judaism, Maimonides is the one who expresses most clearly the idea of free choice, and makes a massive effort philosophically to reconcile man's free choice with the determinism which exists in nature. And the other great believer in the Jewish world (who, according to not an exactly correct categorization prevalent today, is said to be more orthodox than Maimonides), R. Hisdai Crescas, denies free will— and both were men of faith. And in the world of philosophy which does not know of God, two great men of the new philosophy argue over this. Kant, the atheist, makes a mighty effort, and constructs an unsurpassed edifice, in order to reconcile the concept of man's free choice with the determinism which is found in nature. On the other hand, the atheist Spinoza adamantly rejects free choice. This is not a dispute between believers and non-believers, but a profound dispute in man's consciousness, which cuts across the camps of the believers and the non-believers.

There are those who claim, for alleged reasons of faith, that we must deduce from the Torah that man has free choice: "I have set before you life and death, blessing and curse: therefore choose life." But one should note that the Torah demands of man to choose the good and to choose life, but does not promise that he has the power to choose. And that, too, is one of the great problems which occupies thinkers on values and ethics: Do religious and ethical demands that man realizes cannot be fulfilled make sense? And on this, too, there is a dispute. There are those who hold that a demand related to faith or ethics has no meaning unless it is in keeping with man's abilities. Others, though, state that there is deep meaning even in those cases where man may be aware that he has been commanded to achieve a certain goal toward which he must strive, even if he knows that he will never attain that goal. He fulfills his obligation by attempting to reach that goal. Here too, there are differences of opinion both among believers and non-believers.

And again, as a hint, I would like to note a late document in the world of Judaism, the *Shulchan Arukh*, whose first word, "One must make a supreme effort"—indicates the enormous magnitude of the demand to get up to serve God. The great believer, the author of *Shulchan Arukh*, was possibly aware—just because of his profound faith—that man is not able in any way to serve God: serving God is something beyond human nature, but man is commanded to attempt to serve God. Therefore this great document of faith, the codex of the laws relating to the service of God, begins with the Hebrew word of "one must make a supreme effort." And if in our *sidra* it states, "choose life," it does not state that man is capable of doing so, but that he is commanded to attempt to choose the good and not the bad, the blessing and not the curse, life and not death.

HA'AZINU

This time I have the great privilege, which is also a great responsibility, to speak before the audience of my listeners and viewers on the day before *Rosh Hashana*. This should have taken precedence over everything else, but the broadcasts are made within the framework of weekly discussions on the Torah *sidrot*, and the next *sidra* to be read will be *Ha'azinu*, which will be read on the day after *Rosh Hashana*. I am therefore refraining from discussing *Rosh Hashana* at length. But one cannot ignore it completely. I will therefore take the liberty of hinting at what I would have discussed, had I been permitted to devote this talk to *Rosh Hashana*.

I would like to pay attention, and draw the attention of the viewers and listeners, to two sections of the *Rosh Hashana machzor*, "*Uvekhen ten pachdekha*" and "*Aleynu leshabeiach*," which embody in the most sublime form man's consciousness regarding the kingdom of heaven and the acceptance of the Yoke of the Kingdom of Heaven, and the expectation that the whole world will accept the Kingdom of Heaven, without any regard for anyone's personal problems, his natural needs, and even the specific problems of the Jewish people. But I will not say anything of the religious folklore of *Unetaneh tokef*, which many naively and erroneously regard as the cardinal subject of *Rosh Hashana*.

Let us get back to *Ha'azinu*. Here, too, I am faced with a special task, for, according to the Hebrew calendar this year, the *Shabbat* on which we read *Ha'azinu* is *Shabbat Teshuva*—the *Shabbat* between *Rosh Hashana* and *Yom Kippur*. Nor can *Ha'azinu* be dealt with exhaustively in a short discussion, and I will restrict myself to a statement in *Sifre*: "This song (i.e., *Ha'azinu*) is great, for it pertains to the present, the past and the future." I could have devoted myself entirely to this statement, but will not do that either.

Shabbat Teshuva, which is the preparation for *Yom Kippur*, and *teshuva*—both as concept and as action—are among the basic components of religious consciousness. This *Shabbat* is also referred to as *Shabbat Shuva*, based on the first word of the *haftara* in Hosea which we read this year with the *sidra* of *Ha'azinu*. It seems to me that one cannot doubt the fact that when Hosea began with the great call: "Return O Israel to the Lord your God, because you have fallen by your iniquity" (*Hoshea* 14:1), he was thinking of the short *parasha* before *Ha'azinu*, which I had the privilege to speak about last week, the short *parasha* of *teshuva* (*Devarim* 30:1–10). I have no doubt that when Hosea phrased his call in the form of "Return O Israel to the Lord your God," he had before his eyes the statement by Moses: "You will return to the Lord your God."

Not only does Hosea call for repentance, but he also foresees the repentance in the future. He presents it in a most beautiful way, as man's elevation to the highest peak, to the true spiritual joy, and he designates it for Israel—and here he is referring to the kingdom of Ephraim, which he mentions by name, or, in other words, the ten tribes. Here we have one of the most sublime of prophecies, which was not fulfilled, and we know that it will not be fulfilled, for, unlike what Hosea had foreseen, Ephraim and all the ten tribes disappeared off the face of the earth. In no sense did they return: they did not return to God in repentance, and they did not return to their land and their birthplace after their exile. We have already discussed this on a number of occasions, and here it is presented in the most clear fashion, that a prophet only prophesies as to what should ideally take place, but that gives us no guarantee that this will actually take place. The words of the prophets are not oracles for the future, but indicate a purpose and a goal for which we must work and for which we must strive—whether it is realized or not. This vision, and our striving to attain it, are themselves of the highest religious value.

I would like to pause at the last verse in Hosea's prophecy. After the call for repentance and the vision of the repentance which must come, Hosea concludes with the verse, "For the ways of God are straight, and the righteous walk in them: but the wicked stumble in them." This verse can be read simply without any great thought, but one should give it great thought. "For the ways of God are straight, and the righteous walk in them: but the wicked stumble in them"— in what do they stumble? In the ways of God. Here we are told something tremendous: the very walking in the ways of God, in the ways which God orders man to go, is no guarantee that man is not sinning. Everything depends on his intention and aim. A person can walk in the ways of God not because he intends to go in His ways, but because he regards walking in God's ways as a means to satisfy some need or needs. And here one should not differentiate between a personal need and a public, national or universal need. Even a sinner can walk in the ways of God if he expects profit from doing so—and he still remains a sinner.

This is one of the most profound notions in religious awareness, and not everybody is capable of understanding it. The ancient *Targum* is taken aback by what the verse says, and interprets it in a way which removes it from its *peshat*. This is the way the *Targum* translates the verse: "'the righteous walk in them'—the righteous who walk in them will gain life in the world to come." The *Targum* does not comprehend that the nature of the righteous is that he walks in the ways of God because he sees that as man's purpose, but rather regards walking in the ways of God as a means to receive the reward of the world to come. But the second part is more important: "'but the wicked will stumble in them'—the wicked persons will inherit

hell because they did not walk in these ways." The *Targum* does not
see the evil consisting of a person not walking in the ways of God,
but rather in that a person will inherit hell because he did not walk in
the ways of God.

But Hosea is speaking clearly of a wicked person who is walking
in the ways of God. This is exactly what we read, in a more profound formulation, in the *vidui*—confession—which is said on *Yom
Kippur*, according to the Sephardic rite, in which—in enumerating
the sins for which a person requests God's forgiveness on *Yom
Kippur*—it states: "we have performed *mitzvot* not for the service of
God." We have performed the *mitzvot*—but this is considered
among our sins, if we did not do them for the service of God.

The *haftara* of *Shabbat Teshuva*, and what is recited in the *vidui*
on *Yom Kippur*, for which *Shabbat Teshuva* is a preparation, are
among the great matters which many who consider themselves
believers do not understand. Faith and the worship of God, and the
observance of the *mitzvot*, are not something utilitarian, but are
values in themselves. The righteous person is one who walks in the
ways of God—and nothing is said about what is accomplished by
doing so beyond the walking itself. The wicked person may indeed
walk in the ways of God, but if he does not recognize that walking
in His ways is the purpose and the goal, but rather sees it as a means
for himself, or even for the Jewish people, he remains a wicked
person. And that is something very important in understanding the
Ten Days of Repentance.

KOHELET
(for the Intermediate Shabbat of Sukkot)

The *megilla* of Ecclesiastes, which is read—according to a *minhag* which has no basis in early *halakha*—on the intermediate *Shabbat* of the festival of *Sukkot*, and, according to one of the *minhagim*, as instituted by the Gaon of Vilna (that of the Ashkenazic rite) is read from a scroll and is preceded by the blessing: "...who has hallowed us with His *mitzvot* and commanded us concerning the reading of the *megilla*," is one of those books whose significance as part of Holy Writ, and in terms of its location within the Bible, has aroused problems from ancient times to this day.

We know from the talmudic sources—already from the Mishna, and even more from the Talmud and the Midrash—that there were doubts as to whether Ecclesiastes (as well as a number of other books) is considered to be Holy Writ. Regarding Ecclesiastes, we are told that there were those who saw in it statements that tend toward heresy and apostasy. But it is very significant that in the end, Ecclesiastes was accepted as one of the books of the Bible. This discussion, which took place in the world of the oral Torah 1,800 years ago, exists in our days as well. Among those who study and interpret the Bible, both Jews and non-Jews, a view exists that this book is a document reflecting religious doubt and a weakening of faith, some even say of clear heresy, which a later editor, who was afraid of these ideas, attempted to rectify, and that was why he added, after the words of seeming apostasy and of clearly expressed doubts, the verse, "The conclusion of the whole matter: Fear God, and keep his *mitzvot*: for this is the whole of man" (*Kohelet* 12:13).

As opposed to this view, I feel adamantly that this book is—on the contrary—a document of the greatest and most profound faith, faith which is not dependent on the conditions in which man finds himself or man's fate in the world—faith "for its own sake," and, following this, the worship of God "for its own sake" and not for any utilitarian purpose or benefit that a person will derive from it. Ecclesiastes recognizes that faith and the worship of God are not "utilitarian" and do not "benefit" one, but as one who believes in God, he accepts upon himself the worship of God, not as a means to support his existence, but as the purpose for human existence.

"Fear God, and keep His *mitzvot*: for this is the whole of man" does not in any way answer the questions: "what is good for man," "what advantage is there for man," etc., which are the questions with which Ecclesiastes struggles throughout the book—until he reaches the above conclusion.

Faith for its own sake is faith in God in terms of acknowledgment of His Godhead, and not in terms of the functions attributed to Him in relation to human needs and desires. Ecclesiastes' religious decision is close to that of Abraham when he went to the *Akeida*, and that of Job at the end of that book: except that Abraham and Job were tested by God, whereas Ecclesiastes withstood the test which he imposed upon himself, in his contemplation and in his doubts.

The major topic of the first eleven chapters and the beginning of the last chapter of Ecclesiastes is the question, "what is good for man," or—in other formulations—"what contributes to man," or "what advantage is there to man," etc., where the "good" and the "advantage" are viewed in terms of satisfying man's natural needs and urges, to make his life more comfortable and to bring pleasure in his life, as a natural creature. And here Ecclesiastes appears to us a nihilist: he does not find in human existence and in the entire world anything which is "good" or "an advantage" for man, for all is vanity. He does not find this in any material achievement, nor in any intellectual achievement, nor in the worship of God in terms of the supposed benefit it brings to man.

The antithesis of the question which is asked repeatedly—what is good for man, for which the answer given is that nothing can be found that is "good" for man—is the last verse, in which we are *not* told what is *good for man*, but what is *the whole of man*, namely, what the meaning is of man's existence in a world where nothing is good for man—this antithesis proves that the last verse is not the addition of a God-fearing Jew who was afraid of the doubts and the heresy in the ideas of the author, but the opposite: this verse expresses the major concept of the author. Ecclesiastes does not say, "Fear God, and keep his *mitzvot*: for this is *good for man*," but in a striking and demonstrative manner, he states, "for that is *the whole of man*." This is comprehension of faith and of the worship of God as values in themselves, not as means to obtain benefits.

Should the reader claim that it would seem that Ecclesiastes, too, gives a utilitarian motivation for fear and worship of God—"For God brings every deed into judgment" (*Kohelet* 12:14)—it has already been explained in the previous chapters that Divine judgment does not refer to a reward given to the righteous for his righteousness or to the wise for his wisdom, nor as a punishment to the wicked for his wickedness and to the fool for his foolishness—for objectively the fate of all of them is the same: "There is one event to the righteous, and to the wicked" (*Kohelet* 9:2), and, "As it happens to the fool, so it happens even to me" (*Kohelet* 2:15). But the reward is the very fact that the person is righteous or wise before God and the punishment is being wicked or foolish before God—and compare this to the passage in the *Nei'la* service of *Yom Kippur*: "Man has no preeminence above a beast" (*Kohelet* 3:19), but "You have from the start separated man and recognized him to stand before You."

This is the way Ecclesiastes portrays all human values, which he regards in terms of their significance in themselves, as ends and not as means. Ecclesiastes displays in a clear fashion the superiority of wisdom over foolishness as, "the superiority of light over darkness," even though, "One event happens to them all...as it happens to the fool, so it happens even to me" (*Kohelet* 2:13–15). Thus we see that the superiority of wisdom is not that it imparts "good" to man in the utilitarian sense, but its superiority lies in it itself—that the person is wise and not foolish. The same idea is to be found in regard to wickedness: "God cares for the pursued (in my opinion, the most probable translation of a verse of doubtful meaning).... God judges the righteous and the wicked" (*Kohelet* 3:15–19). But Divine judgment does not guarantee the victory of righteousness over wickedness: "I saw under the sun the place for justice, that wickedness was there; and the place of righteousness, that wickedness was there...and the same thing befalls them." Rather, the fact of being righteous, that is the superiority of a person.

But the major idea is how Ecclesiastes relates to the fear of God. The *megilla* contains numerous verses which portray the greater worth of those who fear God, and "that it will be well with them that fear God," and "it will not be well with the wicked" (*Kohelet* 8:12, 13). But this "good" is not necessarily reflected in one's objective existence. Ecclesiastes knows that, "there are just men, to whom it happens according to what is due to the wicked; again, there are wicked men, to whom it happens according to what is due to the righteous.... All things come alike to all: there is the same event to the righteous, and to the wicked" (*Kohelet* 8:14; 9:2). And nevertheless—and possibly just because of this—the superiority of the righteous person lies in that he is righteous: God knows that he is righteous.

The superiority of the wise man is that he is wise, and that he is on a higher level than the fool; the superiority of the righteous man over the wicked one is that he is righteous; the superiority of the God-fearing man over the God-denying is that he fears God. Each of these is an end in itself, and is not a means to satisfy human needs and interests.

Thus we see that Ecclesiastes—which some in their naivete or feigned naivete consider to be a book of religious doubt and heresy—tells us what another chapter in the Bible tells us, and the latter is one that all agree is one of the most exalted expressions of what is known as pure faith—the six verses of the first chapter of Psalms: "Happy is the man who does not follow the counsel of the wicked, nor follows in the way of sinners, nor sits among the scornful. But his delight is in the law of God; and in His law does he meditate day and night." Happy is he—and his happiness is depicted allegorically, in a picture drawn from the plant world: "He is like a tree planted by the rivers of water that brings forth its fruit in its season...." But what is the object of this comparison? "For God knows the way of the righteous"—the righteous is happy because God knows that he is righteous: he has merited God's recognizing him as a righteous man, and there is not a word here on what will happen to him objectively. Similarly, "The wicked are not so: but are like the chaff driven by the wind." Again, this is a picture drawn from the plant world, but to what is the comparison? "The way of the wicked is doomed." The wicked walks in a way which is, in itself—not in terms of where it leads to—destruction.

Ecclesiastes, which is regarded as the book of religious doubt, says what the book of Psalms, the book of pure faith, says: that the fear of God and the worship of God are significant in themselves, without relating to the question of the utility or the benefit in them. And thus we understand the exalted end of Ecclesiastes, "The conclusion of the whole matter: Fear God, and keep his *mitzvot*: for this is the whole of man" (*Kohelet* 12:13).

VEZOT HABRAKHA

I have had a great privilege in the year that we will complete tomorrow, the year of the Torah cycle reading, where I was given the opportunity and permission to say something each week on the *sidra* that would be read that *Shabbat*. I have also enjoyed a large audience of listeners and viewers, from whom, from the reactions which have reached me, in writing as well as orally, I learned that some of my words were heard and elicited attention among people.

In *Vezot Habrakha*, the Torah ends with the death of Moses. Today too, within the framework of the few minutes we have, we will not be able to do more than make some comments on the great *sidra* of Moses' blessing to the Jewish people before his death and burial. Of the blessings which Moses gave to all the tribes of Israel, I would like to pause at only one, because from it we are able to draw conclusions of tremendous actual significance: the blessing to the tribe of Benjamin, which, in terms of style is very difficult, and whose literal meaning is not certain. Benjamin is referred to as the beloved of God, and we are told that, "he dwells in security...he (or He?) dwells between his shoulders."

The traditional commentaries—and here we are not sure whether this is the literal meaning or Midrash—refer these words to the fact that the Temple on Mount Moriah was in the territory of the tribe of Benjamin—and if the Temple is the dwelling place of God's glory, then It dwells between Benjamin's shoulders. But this raises a question. It states "He covers (i.e., shields and protects) him the whole day long." The whole day long? Which day? The meaning of the verse is not for a 24 hour day; God's day is eternity. Thus this implies that God's dwelling place is eternal—yet we see that it was not eternal: the Temple was destroyed and the place where it had stood was desecrated, and now a foreign temple stands there. But there is an astounding Midrash (in *Midrash Pitaron HaTorah*, which was only edited for the first time a few years ago). This is a Midrash of the time of the *Geonim* (approx. 500–900 A.C.E.), which has much material from other *midrashim* with which we are familiar, but also contains *midrashim* with which we are not familiar, or were taken from sources that have been lost to us. And in this Midrash, we find a comment on "he (or: "He") covers him the whole day long; he (or: "He") dwells between his shoulders." It states that this prophetic blessing of Moses did indeed come to pass, for the Temple which stands there today, the Temple of another religion, is not a place of idolatry. This temple is one of a religion which acknowledges the unity of God, and which worships God, even if it did not receive the Torah and does not worship God through the observance of the *mitzvot*. Thus we find that it is still a temple for those who truly worship God. This was said at the time of the *Geonim*, at a time when the Muslims ruled Palestine, and the Midrash certainly precedes the Crusades, in which the control of the Temple Mount passed over to those who do not believe in the unity of God, according to our understanding of it.

And now something on the last verse in the Torah, with which we will complete our talks. The last verses of the Torah are the story of the death of Moses and his burial. At the beginning of the *sidra*, Moses is referred to as "the man of God": "This is the blessing, that Moses the man of God blessed..." whereas after his death he is referred to as "the servant of God": "So Moses the servant of God died there in the land of Moab, according to what God said. And he buried him in the valley." Who buried him? And there is a Midrash which is almost astounding, based on the fact that the *gematria*

equivalent of the Hebrew word "in the valley" is 15, and that is the same as God's name, *Yah*: God Himself buried him, "but no man knows of his burial place to this day."

The Torah eulogizes Moses: "There has never yet risen in Israel a prophet like Moses, whom God knew face to face;" and the last verse mentions "all the mighty deeds and all the terrifying acts which Moses performed in the sight of all Israel."

We know the great deeds that Moses did before the eyes of Israel. We know of the plagues of Egypt, of the splitting of the Sea of Reeds, of Israel being taken out of Egypt, of the *manna* falling, of the bringing down of the Tablets of the Covenant. *Rashi*, who completes his commentary on the Torah with a comment on this verse, chooses to use the words of a Midrash:

> "All the mighty deeds, and all the terrible acts which Moses performed in the sight of all Israel"—that he dared to smash the tablets before their eyes, as it states, "and I broke them before your eyes" (*Devarim* 9:17), and God agreed with him, saying, "the tablets you broke" (*Shemot* 34:1)—"which" implies "may your strength increase" (a pun on the phonetic similarity between the Hebrew terms for "which" and for "strengthen").

Thus, the greatest deed that Moses accomplished was not the deliverance from Egypt nor transmitting the Torah, but that he broke the tablets that had been engraved by God, when the people worshipped idolatry, and the holy words given on these tablets might have been desecrated. To break idolatry, not to sanctify values which stem from human drives and interests—that is faith. The main thing in faith in God is not to believe in anything which is not Divine, not to sanctify things which stem from the drive, interests, plans and ideals, and visions of man, even if, in human terms, they are the most lofty of matters. When these things are made into something holy, they are to be smashed.

And that was the greatness of Moses, the man of God, the servant of God, to whom were given the tablets "engraved by God," and which he smashed to show that no object is holy. If those to whom the object is designed do not have the intention of worshipping God, but their own gods, the sanctity may even turn into a stumbling block—and that is a highly important matter.

We are today witness to a terrifying phenomenon that those who are considered to be in charge of dealing with the Torah, and of seeing to the observance of the Torah, use in their statements formulations such as "the sanctity of God and the sanctity of the nation and the sanctity of the land," in the same breath, in a trinity of holiness; these are the same tablets which were given to the people who said of the calf, "these are your gods O Israel" (*Shemot* 32:4). The holiness of God alone—that is the content of faith. If one adds to it the holiness of the nation and the holiness of the land, in one breath and in the same context, the holiness turns into its opposite. And this great example was shown to us by Moses when he smashed this counterfeit and distorted holiness.

About the Author

Professor Yeshayahu Leibowitz, an acclaimed scientist and Judaica scholar, is renowned for his widely respected—and debated—approach to Jewish tradition and philosophy. He served as Editor-in-Chief of the *Encyclopedia Hebraica* and was head professor of the science department at the Hebrew University. Born in Riga in 1904 and educated in Germany and Switzerland, he immigrated to Israel in 1935 and passed away in Jerusalem in 1994.